LIFE IN HANOI

Local and expat stories in Vietnam's capital

PAM SCOTT

First published in Australia in 2005 by
New Holland Publishers (Australia) Pty Ltd
Sydney • Auckland • London • Cape Town

14 Aquatic Drive Frenchs Forest NSW 2086 Australia
218 Lake Road Northcote Auckland New Zealand
86 Edgware Road London W2 2EA United Kingdom
80 McKenzie Street Cape Town 8001 South Africa

Scott, Pam.
Life in Hanoi : local and expat stories in Vietnam's capital.

ISBN 1 74110 214 6.

1. Employment in foreign countries - Anecdotes. 2. Aliens -
Vietnam. 3. Hanoi (Vietnam) - Social life and customs. 4.
Hanoi (Vietnam) - Description and travel. I. Title.

915.97

Publisher: Fiona Schultz
Editor: Jacqueline Blanchard
Internal design: Karl Roper
Cover design: Joanne Buckley
Production Controller: Linda Bottari
Printed in Australia by McPherson's Printing Group, Victoria

Foreword

I had lived in Vietnam from April 1994 until April 2002. At the end of those eight years I had a strong feeling that it was time to go back to Australia. My parents weren't getting any younger and I felt the need to catch up with children and old friends. I wanted to be around people who had known me for a long time. It was a rather strange time, that homecoming. I experienced a kind of reverse culture shock, discovering that I didn't easily fit back in to my own culture. I couldn't find a job and felt like I was just perched in Sydney, ready to take off again sometime in the future. To keep me busy, and as a way of dealing with the emotions I was experiencing about leaving Hanoi, I wrote a book about my adventures and some of the people I met during those eight years. I was lucky enough to find a publisher straight away. My first book, *Hanoi Stories* was published by New Holland in 2004.

A year after I arrived in Sydney my father passed away, quickly and painlessly, after being diagnosed with lung cancer. I had been able to spend a good year with him beforehand, was with him when he died and was able to help my mother get settled into her new home. Then unexpectedly, I received an email from a Vietnamese friend in Hanoi with a job proposal for me to consider. It was a short-term contract, requiring an international project management consultant for a Norwegian Government-funded project supporting education for ethnic minorities in Dien Bien Province for forty-five consulting days spread over four or five months. At first it seemed too hard to uproot myself for such a short period. But, as I thought more about it, I started to see it as an opportunity to move on. I felt as though the gods had allowed me eighteen months respite to carry out my family responsibilities in Australia, but were calling me back to finish whatever it was I was meant to do in Vietnam.

There was no longer any real reason for me to stay in Australia. I had no job and I had finished writing my book. I did have ideas for other stories I wanted to write and even thought about trying my hand at filming. Vietnam was such a rich source, barely tapped, and I had entry to it. A part-time job in Hanoi was perfect for what I wanted to do. Once the decision was made I quickly packed my few personal possessions and stored them with friends, sold the few bits of furniture I'd acquired, sold my car and headed off to Hanoi one more time. But, was I leaving home or going home? I didn't know any more.

As it turned out the consultancy was extended beyond the original finish date of early 2004 and I was invited to stay on until the project ended in 2005. It seemed that the gods were still not willing to let me leave, but by now I was committed to writing this book and so it suited me well to extend my stay.

Originally, I had the idea to write the stories of other expats, like myself, who had found themselves in Hanoi or had taken deliberate steps to invent a life for themselves in the city. I wasn't interested in the diplomats, or the international career men and women who were largely sent somewhere and told what to do, and often lived a fairly privileged existence in foreigner enclaves. Over the years I had met some truly delightful, amazing and inspiring people doing all sorts of things on their own initiative and I wanted to tell their stories.

I wanted to inspire readers with the notion that you didn't have to be brilliant or famous or have some unique talent to try living in a completely different culture. A motor mechanic, a nurse, a jewellery shop owner, a lawyer, a travel agent, a sailor, a teacher, someone just like themselves or their neighbour could have a life-changing adventure. All it required was the desire and a little courage to step out into the unknown and dare to be different.

So, I went around Hanoi armed with my new digital voice recorder to talk to these ordinary and extraordinary men and women who had made Hanoi their home and asked them to share their own Hanoi stories. They agreed generously and fearlessly and I thank them so much for their trust. I covered a range of ages, nationalities and backgrounds of both men and women, to try to make sure there was at least one story that might make a reader think 'that could be me!'

Before I started on the stories of the other foreigners in town, I needed to record my own feelings about coming back and this led me to re-discover some of the Vietnamese who inhabited my Hanoi world, who were ordinary/extraordinary in their own way. And so my story in this collection is really their stories and how their lives have interwoven with my Hanoi life.

Contents

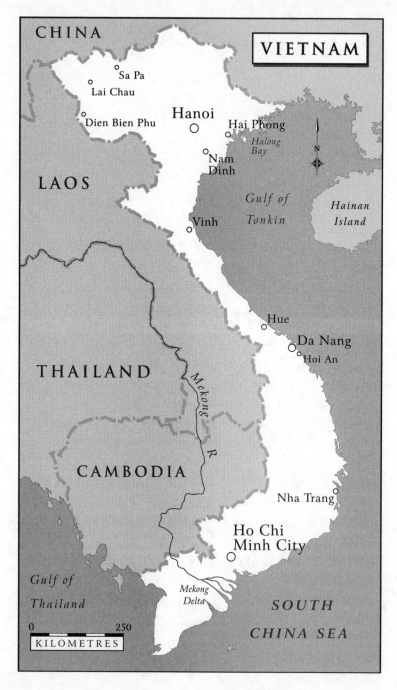

Pam's Story:
Return to Hanoi

'*Lau lam* (long time),' they said rather nonchalantly at the noodle shop.

'I've been looking for you,' said Miss Nga, formerly a housemaid at the Post Office Guesthouse where I lived for almost three years, as she grabbed me outside a clothing shop.

'You look the same,' said Giang, a former work colleague, leaving me unsure whether she was surprised or disappointed. It was as if I had never left. At the little rice eatery on Nguyen Du Street they immediately served up my normal lunch order without me having to say a word. The past eighteen months in Australia disappeared as if only a dream. Returning to Hanoi was like putting on an old pair of comfortable shoes, Like meeting an old friend and slipping back easily into the old patterns. Everything came flooding back—street names, people's names, even the language. Maybe the fortune tellers were right when they told me that Vietnam was like a holy place, a fairy-land for me.

The rate of change had been extraordinarily rapid over the years since I first visited in 1993, especially in the late 90s, and I had expected to find that these changes had continued during my absence. But, I was surprised to find that at least in the centre of Hanoi things remained much the same. There were many more cars and motorbikes and consequently more traffic jams, noise and air pollution, but large-scale building in the centre of the city seemed to have tapered off. The tourist shops were still selling the same lacquer and bamboo, silk and embroidery products. There were a few more up-market art galleries but the pavements were still cluttered with various street vendors, the *xe om* drivers still clustered on every street corner, the bread sellers still carried hot bread rolls in a basket on their head, calling for customers. One thing that certainly hadn't changed was the difficulty I had finding a small, reasonably priced apartment near the centre of Hanoi. My friend suggested I call Mr Long, a real estate agent specialising in accommodation for foreigners. I'm afraid I lost confidence in Mr Long when he told me he had a good place for me that turned out on inspection to have no windows! 'But it's very cheap,' Mr Long explained. 'Not when I take into account my doctor's bill, when I go crazy,' I replied. Mr Long lost a bit of interest in me after that—clearly I was too demanding. Thankfully, Mr Kien, from a rival real estate firm, had a better idea of what foreigners want in a flat

The place I decided upon was on the first floor of what had previously been a mini-hotel and was now converted into apartments. Mine had a spacious bedroom with a large wooden bed, wardrobe, a reasonable-sized bathroom and a large airy living room with a kitchen bench along one wall and large windows that looked out into the tree-tops. Of course it was the windows that sold me. They even made up for the stink of cigarette smoke that permeated the carpet, curtains and fabric lounge. As it turned out, I had to leave Hanoi for a week, returning two days after the current tenant moved out. Perfect timing for having the place aired and freshened up. The owner agreed to give it a fresh coat of paint and a good clean. There was even the possibility that she might replace the tatty living room curtains with vertical blinds so I could make the most of my leafy treetop aspect.

I checked out what had been done in my absence before moving my belongings in. I knew the painting had been done as soon as I opened the door. Not by the smell, but by the large splashes of white paint on the grey carpet at the front door. Paint drips and splotches could be found on most of the furniture. One advantage of the extremely ugly and very shiny furniture that abounds in rental accommodation in Hanoi is that the paint spots soon wore off the slippery surface! There was still a bit of a smell of smoke although they had clearly tried to air out the place, but on the windows, no curtains—and no sign of any replacement either. As I pointed to the bare windows, Tien, the young man from the office downstairs who managed the building, scurried away. This wasn't looking promising. But a couple of minutes later he was back with two sets of swatches for me to select the colour I liked for the vertical blinds. I had been too hasty in my judgement. I was wondering how long I would have to wait in this fully exposed state, shielded only by the leaves of my tree from my neighbours across the narrow road. 'This afternoon', said Tien. Oh sure! I thought. My mother had recently ordered some similar blinds in Sydney and the measuring, making and installation process had taken weeks. Of course, in typical Hanoi style I was proven wrong. That afternoon when I arrived back from shopping, two men were putting the finishing touches on my brand new blinds. I was so excited and surprised that I didn't notice at first that at one end they were too long and dragged along the sill. I pointed this out to Tien. A few days after, I came home to find the same two men up a ladder with scissors rectifying their mistake.

In direct contrast to finding a place to live, actually moving in is a breeze in Hanoi. It helped that I didn't have many possessions this time, but even in the past when I had moved a billiard table and drum kit from house to house it was still relatively painless. Someone is always available to help carry things and trucks of varying sizes are available at fifteen minutes notice. Mr. Tien came along to help me with the bags I had left with my friend and in no time I was getting settled in to my new home, looking forward to a quiet afternoon of unpacking and arranging my belongings.

Suddenly, the calm of my room was shattered. A man with an enormous electric masonry drill was ushered in by Tien and started drilling the wall of my bedroom near the airconditioner. It had been leaking and now they decided to put a hose through the wall to take the excess water away. After two hours of ear-splitting noise all I had was a huge hole in my bedroom wall, a pile of dust and rubble on the carpet and a trail of muddy water down the wall. Of course, after a couple of hours of use, the airconditioner still leaked, requiring the workers to come back another day and try to patch up the mess. Then the phone wouldn't work and Tien was running around trying different handsets and later wrapping clear sticky tape around bent wires. At this point, feeling a little uptight, I realised that I hadn't completed my re-adjustment to Hanoi. Why, I asked myself, should I take for granted that things always work, that a bath would be installed so that all the water drained out the plughole instead of leaving a shallow pool at the opposite end? I needed to change my expectations and keep things in perspective, and more importantly I needed to rediscover my sense of humour.

This was a timely reminder because I was about to head off for a week in the distant north-western city of Dien Bien Phu, scene of the famous military battle where the French colonists were finally routed by the Vietnamese in 1954. The job that brought me back to Vietnam required that I spend a week in Dien Bien Phu every two or three weeks for a total of nine weeks. A week in Dien Bien Phu meant staying at the Muong Thanh Hotel, considered the best in town, where a sense of humour and revised standards were, I discovered, going to be essential survival skills.

Nothing at the Muong Thanh Hotel was installed correctly or worked properly. On my first trip to Dien Bien Phu I didn't realise that I had been given the best room in the hotel. On my second visit the Norwegian Ambassador and a Norwegian government minister came along and were given the best rooms while I was sent off to another building. On first glance the room they gave me looked okay, even though it had three beds. As I started to unpack I found that the lamp was broken so I took a globe to reception to be replaced. Then I tried the airconditioner and millions of ants came falling out of it! The sheets on the bed below were black with the bodies of ants, and so too the bedside table and floor. It sounded like rain, there were so many ants falling. A young man who worked there tried to clean them all away. He sprayed and wiped and took the front panel off the airconditioner, but the supply of ants seemed endless and they were immune to the insect spray that was leaving me unable to breathe. Next we found that the control on the airconditioner didn't work, leaving the choice for the night between icy cold or steamy hot. Finally it was decided I should move to another room.

The hotel worker checked the new room: no ants here and the airconditioner worked. After he left I found that the lamp didn't work and none of the windows or doors shut properly. I improvised, not wanting to complain any more. I managed to tie some of the windows closed with small towels and used a comb, wedged inventively, to keep the bathroom door closed. It was important to keep the door closed because the bathroom window was permanently open, allowing what I feared might be malaria-bearing mosquitoes to come in and also a rather disgusting smell, a combination from the sewerage system and the poultry yard beneath. The first room I was given had lots of coathangers in the cupboard but no rail to hang them on. The second room had a rail but no coathangers! The doors and windows all had the same semi-transparent curtains with fringes and tassels, smocking and flounces, clearly requiring many metres of material.

However, in what I could only imagine as an attempt to economise after the extravagance of the curtains, there was only one sheet per bed, a strange piece of material with raw frayed edges. Instead of a pillowcase there was just a rectangular piece of material that lay on top of the pillow.

When the Norwegian delegation left, I was moved to my old room, the same room that on my first visit I thought was pretty poor. Now, it felt like luxury, the familiar wet feet when you used the hand basin, the black things living on the ceiling, the mould and dirt on the walls, the sagging mattress, the fluorescent light that sounded like a compressor, the power points that were falling off the wall, a bedside lamp that needed to be jiggled and cajoled into life.

The real talking point of the Muong Thanh Hotel is the statuary outside. Near the reception entrance are statues of the characters from *Monkey Magic*. Monkey, Pigsy, Sandy and the Buddhist monk on a white horse stand in procession. Near the large bamboo and thatch restaurant, capable of holding three or four hundred guests for wedding celebrations, its entrance flanked by two life-sized knights in armour astride their steeds, is a large square-shaped but rather shallow pool with a tableau of bizarre wild life on its edges: a life-size giraffe family, a penguin family, two ostriches, a Neanderthal couple, deer, Greek statues, a little boy peeing into the pool, a rhino, dragons galore. It is not clear what inspired this vision, but it does provide an interesting feature and is the only swimming pool in town.

While I was in Dien Bien Phu, it was Hanoi that I longed for. That seductive city had quickly worked its charm on me again and I was hooked once more. But it was different this time. For one thing, I had taken off my rose-coloured glasses. When I left Hanoi in 2002 to return to Sydney I was ready to leave, feeling disenchanted with the way I saw the society and people heading. Of course, I was being unrealistic and maybe even deliberately pessimistic in an attempt to soften the trauma of leaving my home of eight years. Then, eighteen months in Sydney brought an awareness of that city's shortcomings, too. Whilst enjoying all Sydney's wonderful attributes—the physical beauty, access to quality entertainment and education, familiar customs and an openness and easiness about living there—I also encountered the annoying negative aspects and a feeling that Australians don't appreciate just how lucky they are. At the same time I started to write a book about my life in Vietnam, which served to remind me of the many wonderful things I had enjoyed, the adventures, the friendships and the many kindnesses.

During this period of seesawing loyalties I finally recognized that you couldn't find all the good points together in one country any more than you could find all the desirable attributes in one person. It's a package deal, the good with the bad. I also realised that like many expats, I now had two homes, two cities where I felt equally but differently comfortable. I had watched my kids and neighbours' kids grow up in Australia, and I had also watched friend's kids and neighbourhood kids grow up in Vietnam. I had taught hundreds of young people in both countries. It gave me a feeling of investing in the future of both places. After only a week or so back in Hanoi I was crossing Lo Duc street at a set of traffic lights. A young policeman was stationed on the other side of the road to warn traffic that the road had been changed to one-way that day. As I walked towards him he said: 'How are you Ms. Scott?' I was amazed and a little alarmed to think the police were keeping tabs on me. Then he took off his sunglasses and smiled at me, 'It's me, Vu, don't you remember?' Of course I remembered Vu. He was the son of Mrs Diep and Mr Dong who owned the hotel in Nguyen Du Street where my friend Anne had once stayed, and where my parents stayed and were treated like royalty. Vu, who as a kid used to play in the lobby, who used to help out in the restaurant his parents later opened on West Lake. Vu, who always spoke English so beautifully and was so polite. Now, here he was, a young man starting his career in the police force.

Hanoi was still up-beat with a palpable energy everywhere, its young population in stark contrast to Australia's greying population of baby boomers. Once I started to look further afield, I found the building boom had moved to the edge of the city in the areas around West Lake, especially near the new Water Park, and a new residential area near the zoo. Palatial homes were being constructed for the nouveau riche of Hanoi, each vying for a view of the lake. And when I looked more closely, I could see evidence of more material affluence in the society. More people carried mobile phones, more luxury goods were available and clearly being bought by locals, not tourists. Where once the better restaurants in town would only have foreign diners, now they were more likely to be filled by Vietnamese. Holiday packages within Vietnam and to neighbouring countries such as China and Thailand were being promoted to Vietnamese with a new disposable income. The rich were clearly getting richer, buying cars instead of motorbikes, filling newly renovated houses with the latest TV, DVD and sound equipment, looking for high quality personal products and clothing and spending money on leisure activities. All this was a far cry from what it was like when I first came to live in Hanoi. In 1994 there were no taxis, few cars, almost no telephones or computers in the entire country, and most people wore plastic shoes and simple clothes and rode bicycles.

Vietnam has struggled for independence for centuries. First it was the Chinese who ruled Vietnam for 1000 years. In the late nineteenth century at the height of the French Colonial period, Indochina became an important French colony. France clearly had ambitious plans for its acquisition and today there are still many French colonial buildings still standing in Vietnam. The French were finally ousted in 1954 following the decisive battle of Dien Bien Phu, where Vietnamese troops under the leadership of General Giap famously hauled cannon and arms using bicycles over the mountains surrounding the plateau of Dien Bien Phu to surprise the French garrison there.

The Vietnam War (or American War as it is known by the Vietnamese) of the 1960s and 1970s exacted a heavy toll from the people, but the following decade brought harder times economically. People were starving and the United States imposed an embargo that prevented any significant international assistance. The fall of the Soviet Union was a further blow to the Vietnamese economy.

For me, living in Hanoi and watching the changes since 1994 has been a fascinating experience and privilege. It was like seeing the development of fifty years in Australia compressed into a decade. Although there had been clear signs of increased affluence and consumerism before I left in 2002, there had been another leap in the intervening eighteen months. Conspicuous consumption had become the order of the day, with the rising middle classes trying to outshine their neighbours with their new modern lifestyle.

Government reports and newspapers in Vietnam painted a glowing picture of the economy for the most part, but every now and then concerns would surface about the widening gap between rich and poor, between city and countryside. This socialist republic was developing into a consumer society divided into 'haves' and 'have nots'. With the rose-coloured glasses taken off it could be clearly seen on any Hanoi street.

Since early 1994 I had been walking along Pho Hue, past a man standing on the corner of Ham Long Street, a bicycle tyre repair man. Every day he would be there with his bicycle pump, a small plastic bowl of water for detecting leaks and repair kit. No matter how early I walked by, he was there. And he stayed there all day until nightfall. In summer he wore a soiled white canvas hat. In winter, he wore a fur-lined Russian-style hat with earflaps to keep the chilly winds that whipped around the corner at bay. His face would light up whenever I said hello as I passed.

The trouble with familiarity is that we tend to accept what we see every day unquestioningly. To me, the man on the corner was just part of the scenery of Pho Hue. But, returning to Hanoi from Sydney and seeing life with new eyes made me wonder about this man. All around him were changes. The traffic along Pho Hue had changed from being predominantly bicycles in 1994 to the madness of cars and motorbikes, where only a few bicycles jostled for space. The shops had changed; in their appearance and in the products they sold. Where once they sold red thermos flasks and Polish electric kettles, they now sold mobile phones and American sports shoes. So, what about his life? I wanted to know. Had it changed in the last decade? On the surface it seemed unchanged. Just day after day of mind-numbing sameness. Or had he in some way that my eyes couldn't detect enjoyed the economic success of the country?

I started to look more carefully as I walked my old neighbour-hoods. The old lady who sold small cups of tea from her street-side stall, the motorbike taxi driver, the noodle man. How, I asked myself, had a decade of prosperity affected their lives? Were there losers as well as winners in this game of economic renovation introduced in 1986, that only really got started in the early 1990s, or was every-one winning, but to different degrees? Maybe I couldn't get reliable answers to these questions, but I at least wanted to understand the people who populated my world on the streets of Hanoi; people whose names I may not always know but who were clearly etched in my mind as an important part of the city landscape.

Mr Hieu
bicycle repairer

Mr Hieu, I discovered, has been standing on the corner of Pho Hue and Ham Long streets waiting to repair bicycles for thirty years, much longer than the ten years I have seen him there. He has lived in the same house just a few doors away for fifty years. Mr Hieu was born in Hanoi in 1937. His father worked on the railways during the

French colonial era but both parents died when he was quite young. He had an older sister who got married when Hieu was in the Army. After that he didn't want to bother her life, as she had a family of her own to look after. So, following his three years of Army service Hieu went back to his small room in Pho Hue and has lived there alone ever since.

Every day is much the same. Hieu gets up at 5 a.m. to exercise. He walks to the corner ready to start work at 6.30 a.m. or 7 a.m. and stays there until 6.30 p.m. After dinner he sometimes goes for a walk, around Hoan Kiem Lake or to a nearby park, or watches TV. Occasionally, if he feels like it, he might finish work early. Every day Hieu has watched the world of Hanoi change before his eyes while his own life remains unchanged and unchanging. And yet, far from being resentful or depressed about this, Hieu appears youthfully optimistic, looking forward to a bright future. He even said he might open a small shop one day, although that sounds highly unlikely.

When you ask Hieu if he is married, he replies, 'Not yet.' He attributes his good health to being single. He believes marriage makes you weak. On the other hand, when asked about his hopes for the future Hieu says that maintaining good health and hoping for a happy family are the most important—seemingly irreconcilable goals according to his own philosophy. Since he hasn't managed to get married in more than six decades it seems unlikely that this will happen in the future, and yet it appears he hasn't given up entirely.

According to Hieu he is happy and satisfied with his life. He never expected to get everything, so he is happy with what he has. He tries to do his job a little better each year but even though he is more skilled now, he admits there is less work for him these days and therefore less money. He earns less than US$1 a day. He only has basic tools for repairing bicycles but can do simple motorbike repairs as well. He also does key-cutting these days. Hieu believes he is lucky because he enjoys the same good health as ten years ago and although he recognises that his standard of living is not high, he can manage his life. And that, for him, is enough. There he stands day after day on his little corner of the world, seemingly content, accepting this as his lot in life.

Ms Kim Quy
hairdresser

Kim Quy gave me my first haircut in Hanoi in 1994. At that time she had a tiny shop, not more than about three metres square, in Tran Quoc Toan, opposite the Post Office Guesthouse where I was living. The shop had no glass windows or doors, but was open directly onto the street, so that haircutting and washing, manicures and pedicures were all very public. It was my first introduction to the relaxed and comfortable approach to hair washing and massage in Vietnam. I experienced none of the neck-breaking contortions that I was used to in Australia, sitting in an upright chair with my head pulled back over a sink, a sharp plastic draining board digging into me. In Vietnam you are invited to fully recline on a padded chaise lounge, neck comfortably aligned to the rest of your spine and for fifteen minutes or more you are shampooed and massaged. No wonder Vietnamese women want to go to the hairdresser regularly just for washing. And Kim Quy gave great haircuts. It was only years later that I discovered she was famous in Hanoi and much sought after as a teacher of hairdressing.

Kim Quy was born in Hai Phong in 1952 into a well-off family. Her father was on the management board of a company making agricultural products and her mother on the management board of the power company. But it was her grandparents who were really wealthy. Her grandfather was a construction contractor, her grandmother, to whom she felt closest, a large landowner. As a young teenager, Kim was infected with the patriotic spirit of the nation fighting for independence. The legal age to join the armed forces was eighteen years. When she was just sixteen Kim cut her finger and wrote a letter in blood to the recruitment team begging them to let her join up. The letter was later put on display at the Department of Culture and Information in Hai Phong as an example of devotion to the cause of independence.

Even though her parents were patriotic, her mother burst into tears when she learnt that her two eldest sons and her eldest daughter Kim had signed up for service. Three children from the one family joining up on the same day, one of them a sixteen-year-old girl, made the newspapers of the time. Although it wasn't confirmed until the end of the war, both her brothers were killed and their bodies remain missing.

Kim was sent to Hanoi during her service and became skilled in tracking American planes for the Vietnamese Air Force. From listening to the signals she would draw a map of the aircraft's path onto a glass screen and from this information the Vietnamese forces would know where to fire. This was her task from July 1968 until October 1973. Because of her skill, which eventually gained her the rank of lieutenant and position as head of the information unit, she was always where the fiercest bombing occurred. There were periods where she would work for twenty hours without food or a break. She was also involved in tracking the B52 bombing raid on Hanoi that lasted 12 days and nights. It was certainly a dangerous time to be in Hanoi and more so for Kim's unit since it was a prime target for the Americans. They had to keep moving very quickly to avoid being bombed. Once she heard a BBC radio report that her unit had been destroyed when in fact they had managed to escape just in time. Sometimes she had to sleep out in the open, even in graveyards without shelter, because the villagers knew that if they stayed in the village, the Americans would discover their tracking signals and bomb the place. Kim managed to avoid serious injury, although she did break her collarbone when she had a fall trying to repair a radar antenna. Hardships were ignored in the excitement and in the feeling that a contribution to the fight for independence was being made.

In 1973, after leaving the Air Force, Kim married. Her husband, who was six years older, had left the Air Force four years earlier and gone to study engineering at university. Now, they were both free to start married life in Hanoi in a house they had inherited. Whilst they were luckier than many, having a roof over their head, it was still a time of shortages and almost everyone was poor.

Kim became a kindergarten teacher at a government school, looking after children from two months to six years of age. Her own two daughters were born in 1974 and 1976. She worked at this job for six years, taking her girls to work strapped into small seats attached to her bicycle. All this time her husband was working as an engineer at the port in Hanoi. At night they both made candies and biscuits to sell for extra money.

Once she stopped her kindergarten work Kim continued making confectionery until 1983 when she tried tailoring for a while. Next, she opened a café on the ground floor of their home, but her younger daughter (who remembers nothing of this episode) didn't like her mother doing this work and cried a lot and was angry with customers, forcing Kim to think of an alternative.

It was Kim's next venture that proved to be successful. In 1984, after studying hairdressing for only eighteen days she turned her café into a hairdressing salon and in a very short time developed a reputation in Hanoi for style. The family was still poor so Kim and her husband put together their own version of a salon hairdryer using a plastic basket and a small cheap fan. They made hair curlers by cutting up wooden chopsticks.

Initially Kim took up hairdressing because she thought she could make money from it. But as she understood more about it she realised that she could express her artistic flair in this way, making it a more interesting choice of career. She had always been interested in fashion and was careful about her own appearance. Clothes that her mother bought her when she was young, she would take to a tailor and have altered to her design. She was always different, with her own style. Even during the war she tried to alter her uniform to a more attractive fit—and was punished for her attempt. She was also ahead of her time not just in her hairstyles, but also in marketing strategies. When she first opened her hair salon she hired some beautiful woman (models were unknown in Vietnam at that time) to wear her hairstyles and be seen around town, in the markets and streets, to get people used to something different.

Vietnam had only moved to a market economy in 1986 but already Kim Quy was famous. In 1987 she introduced the concept of branding and had hats made with her name on them. Customers were willing to pay up to twenty times the normal price for a Kim Quy hairstyle. She refers to the years between 1987 and 1991 as her 'golden period', where she gathered fame and fortune.

But, after that time things didn't go so well. In 1992 her marriage broke up and she lost all her savings when someone ran off with all the money she had invested in a private bank. Almost totally broke, she even considered suicide, but instead started again in a small shop in Tran Quoc Toan. By the time I met her in 1994 she was getting back on her feet. Her elder daughter, who resembles her in looks, had been a gymnast and a diver. As she got older and gave up those activities, she too took up hairdressing. Her younger daughter, who took after Kim in spirit, went to study at university in Australia.

In 1996 Kim moved her shop from Tran Quoc Toan to the place where she was living, not far from where she had started her original business, but nothing went right. Rumours spread and competitors who wanted to discredit her said that she was too old now to understand the latest trends for young people. In 1997 she was lucky to earn a dollar a day. This was the worst time in her life.

Then one day, she saw a picture in a western hairdressing magazine of an older person with grey hair standing next to a young student hairdresser in an award ceremony. She realised that she shouldn't worry about giving her skills to others who would then compete with her, and decided to open a training school. Just at that time, she won a scholarship to study for three months in Australia and this gave her the additional skills and confidence that she needed. Over the years, through experience and self-study she had accumulated about half the necessary knowledge of hairdressing. In Australia, she understood how this knowledge was organised into a scientific system and this allowed her to provide high quality training and enhance her reputation. She opened her school in 1998 and within two years had three hundred students. This was the beginning of a new golden age.

Kim's success was not directly attributable to the government's new economic policies in the same way that many fortunes have been made in Hanoi from overseas trade or from providing goods and services to foreigners, but the new environment allowed new ideas to develop and people became more fashion conscious. Kim was able to travel abroad and saw that a more open way of working and sharing knowledge would bring success.

Kim has always been a bit different: from writing letters in blood to adopting revolutionary marketing strategies. Her styles and ideas were often five to ten years ahead of everyone else in Hanoi. She received some criticism and opposition because of this, but over time her vision and creativity have been recognised. These days her life is stable and she is happy knowing that she has overcome the difficulties of her past. She says that her only wishes now are to keep working and for her children to have a smooth life. She recently bought a car and learnt to drive, not something for the faint-hearted given the chaotic traffic in Hanoi. Vietnamese sometimes mistake her for a foreigner, with her up-to-the-minute hairstyles and colours, looking nothing like the other fifty-something matrons of Hanoi. No doubt there is something new percolating away in her brain waiting for the right moment to announce itself.

Mrs Gia
food stall owner

Mrs Gia makes the best *banh cuon* in town! Made of finely chopped pork and mushrooms wrapped in gossamer thin rice sheets and steamed, then sprinkled with fried onions and dipped in a special sauce, this traditional Vietnamese food is a favourite of locals and foreigners alike. Her restaurant consists of a collection of small plastic tables and stools on the pavement of Ba Trieu, a busy main street of Hanoi, that get hidden away whenever there is a police crackdown on unauthorised use of public space. Her kitchen is a small alcove less than two metres square. She sits on a low stool, a small table in front of her loaded with all the ingredients and two large cooking vessels at her side for steaming. During the day she rents this small room to a bicycle seller, but from about 4 p.m. until midnight she serves a stream of hungry Hanoians. And she has been doing it for more than a decade.

Mrs Gia was born in 1952, the Year of the Cat, in Ha Tay province on the outskirts of Hanoi. She studied bicycle making at college and later got a job at a bicycle factory. That's where she met Lap, a young man from Hanoi who had studied economics at college. Lap avoided going into the Army. His two brothers had already become soldiers and Lap's parents argued successfully that their third son should be exempted. Gia became Lap's assistant at the bicycle factory and later his partner in life when they married. In those days in Vietnam there were few job choices and just having enough to eat was a struggle for almost everyone. The war years were difficult enough, but many Vietnamese remember the ten or fifteen years after the end of the

American War as the hardest they endured. By 1985, although they might be employed by the state sector, most Vietnamese were forced to earn a living by 'moonlighting', only keeping their government job for the rations and coupons it provided and possibly some political position and insurance for the future, and finding a second job elsewhere. In 1986 at the Sixth National Party Congress, the Government, recognising that the centrally-planned economy had failed, ushered in a new era of economic renovation with its 'open door' policy. The collapse of the USSR and the loss of its support to the Vietnamese economy hastened the need for further reform. This in turn encouraged entrepreneurs in the private sector. Realising that they would never improve their circumstances if they stayed at the bicycle factory, Gia left her job in 1981 and become successful as a trader in Hanoi. Successful, that is, until something went wrong in about 1988 with her supply chain. Gia was caught with money and goods owed to her on one side and owing money on the other side. It plunged the family into a financial crisis, and as way of earning much needed money, Gia and her mother set up a small eatery. This ran for a couple of years but never very successfully. Then Gia took control and decided to specialise and sell *banh cuon*. Lap left the bicycle factory in 1991 to help his wife run her new business.

Times were hard to begin with and they worried whether they would succeed. But a decade on, Gia and Lap have managed to put their three children through university. Oanh, the eldest daughter, born in 1977, studied marketing at university and is now doing further studies in graphic design. Her younger brother, Linh, studied art at university for five years and is now working for a computer software company. Duong, the youngest girl, graduated from the Languages University and has just started work in the office of the Australian Embassy. All this was managed on the proceeds of *banh cuon*, which sells for just over US twenty cents a plate!

Ms Ha
beauty salon owner

One of the affordable luxuries I discovered in Vietnam was that of having a regular pedicure. These days there is a wide range of choice in Hanoi: you can go to the up-market beauty salons like those at the five-star hotels, initially aimed at expatriates and tourists but recently attracting well-off Vietnamese able to pay the high prices, or you can try the burgeoning number of trendy beauty shops aimed at the young Vietnamese with money to spend. There is an even larger number of established hairdressing salons that offer manicures and pedicures of varying quality at reasonable prices. Then, there are the itinerate practitioners who carry their collection of clippers, files and polishes with them and will perform their service on the pavement or the doorstep of your shop or home if required.

In 1994 went I first arrived I went wandering through the Hom Market near where I was living and decided to try a pedicure. The place I selected was just an open space under the stairs on the ground floor of the market. It had several vinyl-covered lounges for lying down whilst having your hair shampooed, two haircutting chairs in front of large mirrors and some plastic chairs for waiting or having a manicure or pedicure. Using sign language I ordered myself a pedicure.

Ten years later, despite the proliferation of shops available, I still return to this same budget-priced place under the stairs at Hom market. Over the years I tried other places. If I was visiting Nha Trang or working in Saigon, or had moved to a house further away from Hom market I would use the most convenient pedicurist. But I always returned to my old place. They knew me, charged me the correct price and not an inflated foreigner price, made sure they had the nail polish colour that I liked and were always happy to see me— probably their only foreign customer. Ms Ha has been working there almost all that time and is now a part owner of the business.

Ms Ha was born in 1971 in Ba Dinh district of Hanoi, an historic location where Ho Chi Minh announced the Vietnamese Declaration of Independence in 1945. Some of Uncle Ho's ideas about freedom and independence must have influenced Ha many years later because at the age of thirty-four she still chooses to stay single. Ha is the third of five children. Her father worked in a cooperative where he assembled farm machinery and her mother worked for the city's environment and cleaning department. After completing high school Ha stayed at home for some years, helping with household duties. Then, after 1986, change was in the air, heralding new opportunities. Not only was there more money about, at least for some people, but attitudes were changing. Once, only rich people would go to beauty salons. For others it was considered a luxury and a waste of money. But throughout the 1990s an increasing number of people wanted this service and could afford it.

Finding work in this expanding field appealed to Ha and so she set about learning nail care and hairdressing any way she could. There was no class for her to go for training and so she initially taught herself by watching other people working. Then she offered money to a hairdressing salon owner to train her. Luckily, she had a distant relative who took her on as a junior for three years once she had developed some skills. After that Ha opened her own small shop, but when her friend Nhung went to live in Australia, she asked Ha to become a partner and look after her larger and well-established business in Hom market. And that's what she has been doing for the past seven years

Ha enjoys her work. She likes work that requires a number of skills where she can work hard and improve herself. It has certainly helped her improve her life. She earns enough money to be comfortable and although she still lives at home with her parents, following the traditional Vietnamese custom, in other ways she is a modern young woman. Resisting social pressure to marry, Ha remains single despite having many men who are interested in her. She says they don't meet her requirements and she prefers her independence. Increasingly, young Vietnamese women in the major cities are choosing to stay single rather than be pushed into a marriage they don't want. Her choices differ from those of her mother in other ways; for example, she says that if her mother ever had any money to spare she would buy gold to keep for the future whereas Ha likes to use her money to enjoy her life. She can afford to buy nice clothes and accessories and makeup. She enjoys going dancing, something her mother would never have considered. Ha worked hard to learn her trade and she spends long hours at work, from 9 a.m. to 6 p.m. every day. But it isn't as bad as it might seem because these days she can carry her mobile phone with her to the top floor of the market where every day there is ballroom dancing, morning, afternoon and evening. There she can enjoy coffee or other drinks, dance with friends or just enjoy the music. If the shop gets busy she can be contacted on her mobile phone to go back downstairs and work.

Life in Hanoi changed rapidly in the last decade of the twentieth century. The new government policy that opened the door and allowed in modern technology and western ideas changed the culture. Ha was lucky to have choices available to her that would have been unimaginable to her mother's generation, or even a decade earlier. Who can blame her for wanting to make the most of the opportunity to enjoy her life and make it more beautiful?

Mrs Hang
tailor

I had become friendly with Miss Nga, the young receptionist at a nearby hotel, after my friend had stayed there for a holiday. One day

Nga told me she had bought some fabric and was taking it to a famous tailor to have it made into a jacket. I decided that I would try this tailor too and that's how I first met Mrs Hang in 1995. Bui Thi Xuan street is a relatively quiet street between two major roads in Hanoi. Tree-lined, it has a mixture of buildings; some that are French colonial, some art-deco inspired houses, as well as some that are functional cement cubes piled on top of each other for several storeys, some of them small private houses and some that are larger government apartment blocks. Mrs Hang's apartment was on the ground floor of a typically ugly apartment block. The front room served both as the family living room and the place she measured her customers and made them their clothes.

Hang was born in Hanoi in 1951, just a few blocks from where she now lives. Her schooling was cut short because of the war. She remembers having to move back and forth from Hanoi to the rural areas during the bombing raids from 1964 onwards. Her parents stayed in Hanoi and so Hang had to look after her brothers and sisters while they were taking refuge in the countryside. At the same time she made traditional woven bamboo products to sell to help her family. When the bombing raids finally ended in January 1973, Hang settled back down in Hanoi, initially in her parents, home. By then she was married and had three children, a daughter born a few months earlier and twins who were five years old.

Hang met Duong, her husband, when he was the driver in charge of moving the people in her area of Hanoi to safety. After finishing school in 1964 he went to SaPa in the north-western province of Lai Chau for a year as part of a youth brigade serving the war effort. When he was nineteen years old he was sent to Hanoi to join the army and was then sent to China for two years to learn to drive large vehicles used by the army. When he completed his training he returned to Hanoi and drove for the army until 1975. This was dangerous work. A large truck, even using camouflage, was easy to spot from the air and often Duong had to drive at night with no lights. The advantage of this dangerous work was a slightly higher salary and more food coupons for his growing family. Nevertheless, this war period was the most difficult time of their lives.

Once they settled back in Hanoi, Hang and Duong decided to buy the small apartment they still live in. At the end of the war Duong left the army and got work as a driver for a transportation company based in the large northern port city of Hai Phong. After that, he began work driving tourist buses. At the same time as Duong moved to tourism, Hang decided to take up tailoring seriously. She already had some knowledge learnt from her father who made *ao dai*, the long traditional woman's dress, but she decided to go to Ho Chi Minh City for a few months to study modern tailoring techniques and upgrade her skills, leaving her three children in the care of her husband.

The new western tailoring methods and fashions she learnt in Ho Chi Minh City provided Hang with just what she needed to improve her earning capacity and she became well known in Hanoi for her tailoring. From 1985 until 2000 Hang enjoyed successful years. She specialised in cutting and had four or five seamstresses working for her at one time. Her two daughters took up tailoring, following in her footsteps, just as their son followed his father, becoming a tourist driver.

These days Duong is retired, and while it took a bit of getting used to not working, he now enjoys looking after his five grandchildren. Hang stopped sewing for a while in 2001 as her eyes were getting weak and she felt she needed a rest. But, after a lifetime of work she started to miss it and started up again in just a small way by herself. Compared to those early days of marriage when surviving was hard, life for Hang and Duong is comfortable and happy now. Despite Duong's dangerous work during the war he came through it unscathed. In all his years of driving he never had an accident, a record he is deservedly proud of.

Their apartment has been extended and renovated over the years. They have it furnished now in beautiful traditional carved furniture, bought from the family of their son-in law. They are part of the small minority of Vietnamese who follow the Catholic religion and they attend church regularly. Recently, the family invested in a twelve-seat minibus for transporting tourists, with their son as the driver, a means of ensuring enough money for their retirement.

When just having enough food was considered a blessing, fashion and tourism were unheard of luxuries. Style played no part in the struggle for survival and independence. So Hang and Duong were lucky to have acquired the skills at just the right time that allowed them to catch the mounting wave of modernisation. Through hard work they achieved a comfortable retirement and the satisfaction of seeing their children follow in their footsteps.

Mr Suu
chef

Mr Suu has been standing in the same place in Le Van Huu street until 2 a.m. almost every day for more than twenty-five years, cooking the most delicious fried beef and vegetable noodles in Hanoi. And his wife has been standing behind him. When I first went to eat there in 1994, most of the small tables and low stools were ranged along the pavement. Suu, always wearing his brown pork-pie hat in winter and a white cap in summer, was positioned under an awning, his only protection from the weather, with an old wooden bench holding all the ingredients in front of him and a fire at his side. Using the simplest equipment, all his movements were pared to the minimum. Watching Suu cook was watching a true artist at work. He could toss the noodles high over the fire with precision and add herbs and spices with a deft flick of the wrist. Next, he would lightly stir-fry the vegetables, followed by beef cooked in tasty juices and ladled out with a graceful sweep of the arm. The whole delicious mountain of food would be topped off with some garnish and served with a side dish of sliced cucumber. Nothing better on those cold Hanoi evenings, the rising steam thawing cold noses and the generous serving giving a feeling of warm satisfaction inside.

Suu was born in Hanoi in 1947. At age twenty-five, after he finished his years of military service, he went to work in a Chinese restaurant owned by a Hong Kong Chinese woman. Five years later, the Chinese owner went back to Hong Kong and Suu decided to open his own small food shop in nearby Phan Chu Trinh street. Three years after that, when he was thrity-three, Suu married Quy, then twenty-five years old.

Quy was born in Hanoi in 1955, the third of seven children. Her father was a tailor, but he was not strong and life for her family was hard. The children were sent to rural areas for their safety during the bombing of Hanoi in 1967 and 1972. Quy was about eleven years old when she was sent to her mother's village near Hai Duong and she stayed there two years until she completed Class 7 at school. The rural areas were very poor and there was often not enough to eat. Quy remembers having only dry potatoes and no rice to eat a lot of the time. Quy came back and finished high school in Hanoi (at that time Class 10 but these days high school finishes at Class 12) but didn't achieve university entrance so she started work in a garment factory. Even in the years after the end of the war, most people in Vietnam lived day-to-day. Quy weighed only 37 kilograms when she was in her early twenties, but then, she says, everyone else was the same. Most people had not had enough to eat for a long time.

Life improved for Quy when she married Suu. Her parents had died and Suu moved to Quy's family home in Le Van Huu Street and began his food business there with the help of all her family. These days, three generations of Quy's family are still living there and Suu continues to run his food business. Of the seven children, one sister has moved to her own house and one brother is living in Germany. This leaves Quy, one sister, three brothers and all their families sharing the house.

Not everyone in the family is involved in the food business any more, leaving it mainly to Suu and Quy. One of Quy's younger brothers, their sister-in-law and some of their nephews help serve, clean tables and wash dishes on the pavement. Su and Quy's son lives with his grandmother in her house and works as a company driver. Some family members work in hospitals or at the nearby Hom market. But the family still functions as a single unit.

It was a family decision to support Suu when he began his business. It was also a family decision to use their savings to send the third youngest brother to Russia where he earned enough money to go to Germany and become a cook. These days he is well known in Germany as a talented chef and is able to send money back to the family in Hanoi. Thanks to this financial support, in 2003 the family was able to purchase a small parcel of adjoining land and extend their building to house their increasing family numbers, the most recent addition being a little girl born in 2003, the daughter of Quy's youngest brother and a much fussed-over favourite.

Two years ago Suu took ill, possibly a slight stroke as he became paralysed down one side for a time. He seems fully recovered now thanks to the support of his family, many of whom work in hospitals and were able to help him find good treatment. But, for some time the shop was closed and the lack of income and the cost of medical treatment drained them of all their savings. Now, the burden of expensive medicine weighs heavily on the family. Luckily, Suu comes from a family of long-livers. His mother is still going strong at eighty and his great-grandmother lived until she was one hundred and five, receiving a visit and gift of congratulations from Uncle Ho on her one-hundredth birthday. So, maybe there is still plenty of time for Suu and Quy to enjoy the later years of their life.

Suu and Quy have been able to make small improvements in their life by their own hard work and, thanks to help from her brother, the repayment of the family investment years ago of financing him to go abroad. But, their dream of taking a holiday to China, which would cost them US$750 seems as far away as ever. The government's change of policy has had an indirect impact on their economic circumstances. As local people have become better off they spend more on food and eat out more often, but there is also much more competition, too. The young, rich, trendy Hanoians are looking for more style when they dine out. Even the recent renovations at Suu's place have done little more than provide extra indoor space for the same old plastic tables and low stools. Suu himself still uses the same bench I remember from 1994 although he does have a more modern gas cooker now.

Quy's youngest brother has recently come back from Germany where he spent time learning to cook and working in the same restaurant as his older brother. Although he has taken a job selling mobile phones in Hanoi, it is thought that in the future, when Suu can no longer toss noodles, he will be ready to take over the tradition of *pho xau* on Le Van Huu street. Meanwhile Suu and Quy seem quietly resigned to their life and wish only for good health so that they may watch the next generation grow up.

Mr Dzung
motorbike taxi driver

It is only in the last few years that Hanoi has begun to develop a public transport system, beginning with a small fleet of modern buses on a number of different routes with actual schedules. There is even talk of building an underground rail system. In 1993 when I first went to Hanoi there weren't any taxis, let alone buses. The trip from Noi Bai airport into Hanoi at that time took well over an hour along rough roads crowded with some old Russian and Chinese farm trucks, buffalo, motorbikes and bicycles—thousands of bicycles. There were a few private cars for hire at the airport, old Russian 'rust buckets' mainly, and some minibuses owned by fledgling tourist companies. Otherwise, you had to hope that whoever had invited you to Hanoi would come and pick you up in some reliable transport.

The small number of cars on the road at that time was mainly limited to the ubiquitous black sedans of Government and Party officials (usually Mercedes and BMWs), and the white Range Rovers and other four-wheel-drive vehicles of foreign organisations and companies setting up operations in the country. If you didn't have your own bicycle or motorbike to get around the city you hired a *cyclo*. A *cyclo* is like a Vietnamese version of a rickshaw or pedicab, the difference being that the driver sits behind, allowing the passenger an uninterrupted view of what's ahead, not always a welcome prospect! Then a new trend began to spread, that of motorbike taxis, known as *xe om*, where you sit on the back of the motorbike and the driver takes you wherever you want to go for a negotiated price.

When I first came to live in Hanoi at the Post Office Guesthouse, to get around the city I either walked, hired a *cyclo* or else my Vietnamese friends would take me on the back of their motorbikes. But then the *xe om* became more popular. It was certainly faster and more convenient to travel longer distances by motorbike, especially when *cyclos* began to be banned from travelling in some streets in order to improve traffic flow and to make Hanoi appear a more modern city.

I remember clearly the first time I ever used a *xe om*. I had been waiting some time for a *cyclo* to come by, until, fearing that I was going to be late for an appointment, I accepted the offer of a ride from a passing motorbike driver. As soon as I had given him the address and we set off I felt sick with worry. What was I doing riding off into the evening with a perfect stranger who might rob and attack me? Of course, my fears were totally groundless. We pulled up outside the address fifteen minutes later and I paid a modest fee. From then on I became a regular *xe om* user.

At first, Vietnamese were shy about using *xe om*, especially young women, considering it not seemly to be sitting close behind a man they didn't know. But soon it became more common and as this new business boomed, anyone who had a motorbike and no other means of earning money became a motorbike taxi driver. On every corner in Hanoi sat a group of *xe om* drivers waiting to take you wherever you liked.

Mr Dzung became a motorbike taxi driver in late 1995 when he was already thirty-seven years old. As a young man he had spent four years in the Vietnamese Army, during the border war with China. After leaving the army he found a job in a state-owned factory, where he manufactured neon lights. Dzung had expected to stay in his job forever, but the government's new policies in 1986 resulted in the closure of this and many other state-owned factories. The few assets the company had left were divided amongst the employees as a redundancy payment and they were left to find another means of earning a living in a new economic climate.

For the next four years Dzung used his motorbike and travelled north to the Chinese border to become a trader. At first it was easy to earn money this way, but then the government policy tightened and new customs regulations were enforced, making it a risky business. After losing money on one trip, Dzung decided it was much too difficult to continue as a trader. But what could he do to support his wife and two children? His only asset was his motorbike and since his home was located on a busy road, he decided to park his motorbike on the pavement advertising his services as *xe om*.

The street I was living in opened almost directly opposite where Mr Dzung's motorbike was parked, so it wasn't so surprising that I would see his *xe om* sign and use his services one day. What I didn't know until many years later was that he had only just hung his *xe om* sign on his bike the day I did call him to take me somewhere. I was his first foreign customer and almost his first ever customer.

Dzung was embarrassed and ashamed at first to be working as a driver, but he had no alternative. I began to use him regularly. He drove carefully, was friendly and helpful, never tried to overcharge me and looked strong enough to cope with any difficulties that might arise on the road, unlike some of the skinny little drivers around. Even when I moved from Tran Quoc Toan Street I arranged for him to come to my new house and drive me to work each morning and home again in the afternoon five days a week. If I had a special trip, I would sometimes even walk to his place to ask him to drive me there. Slowly, he began to know various details of my life. If I pointed to my hair he knew to take me to my regular hairdresser. He knew where my tailor lived and even where the fortune teller lived, waiting patiently to take me back home again.

Xe om drivers are not likely to become rich. They have to outlay money to purchase and run their motorbike and only ask the equivalent of about US 10 cents per kilometre. When Dzung started, there were not so many motorbike taxis about, but these days there are many more and there is also competition from the new buses. Dzung mainly has old customers now, finding it difficult to attract new ones. The increased traffic on the roads has made the work more dangerous and stressful and the pollution makes it unhealthy, too. As he gets older, he wishes he could stop this work but doesn't know what else he could do. It provides him with enough money to live but little left over to save or for luxuries and entertainment.

Dzung's wife, whom he met when they both worked at the neon light factory, works at a noodle stall belonging to her family. His son, now a teenager, left school early and sells mobile phones, which provides him with enough money for his own life but not enough to contribute to the family. Dzung's daughter is ten years younger and studies well at school and so the family hopes rest on her for the future.

Dzung's house, which formerly belonged to his father, is also where he grew up. The house is small and windowless, consisting of a room downstairs that is only about one and a half metres wide and about four metres long. In it are a refrigerator and a small set of plastic shelves, which hold cooking and eating utensils. There is a set a wooden storage unit holding a TV, video player and music system, some tapes and some glasses and ornaments. On the floor is a woven mat for sitting on. There is a wooden ladder that leads to a bedroom above. Cooking and washing is done in a shared facility outside.

Three generations live here: Dzung's mother, Dzung and his wife, and their two children. From his room, Dzung can look down a tunnel-like alleyway more than 20 metres long to keep an eye on his motorbike and watch for potential customers. His eagle eyes could usually spot me even when I stood on the other side of the busy road. On occasions when he missed seeing me I would go to the alley entrance and shout his name and he would always come.

Dzung expected that after fighting for his country he would have a job for life. But like millions of other Vietnamese caught in the change from a centrally planned economy to a market economy, he found he had to fend for himself by whatever means he could. Had life remained stable and his factory job continued, Dzung believes he may not have had any more money but he is sure he would not have had to work as hard. He may have enjoyed holiday trips with his company and a pension and health care when he retired. Instead, life has been a constant struggle with little time for relaxation. And there seems no end in sight.

Ms Nga
former housemaid

Nga was twenty-three years old when I first met her in 1994. She was one of the housemaids employed at the Post Office

Guesthouse, responsible for cleaning my room and doing washing. A skinny little thing, she rarely complained about the hardships in her life. Instead, she could be heard singing as she performed her daily work, work that earned her US$1 per day at that time.

Nga's parents had met at the Pharmaceutical University when her father was teaching French and her mother was studying to become an analytical chemist. Later, her father went to work at the International Relations Department at Vietnam Post and Telecommunications (VNPT). Nga was the first of three children, followed by a son and another daughter. The family was provided with a university apartment in Lo Duc Street, but the pay for university teachers, like most state employees, was extremely low and so the family was poor. No-one in the family even owned a bicycle. Both her parents walked to work and Nga remembers walking more than five kilometres to school every day. She also remembers always being hungry. 'I was always wanting food and thinking about food. I was envious of anyone I saw with food, especially candy. But the whole city was poor at that time.'

Nga expected that she would attend university having passed the entrance exams, but the untimely death of her father from a cerebral haemorrhage in 1987 at age fifty-three put to rest that ambition. Once she finished high school, Nga knew that she had to do something to help her mother support the younger children, so when she heard about a scheme for sending workers to Russia to work in a garment factory she applied and left Hanoi in 1989 for Moscow. For the first year she had to study Russian language and learn to sew and after that she worked full-time in the factory for another three years. Nga and her mother had hoped that she could earn a high enough salary to support herself and send money back to Vietnam to support the family. However, as it turned out Nga found herself having to earn extra money by trading, selling jeans and T-shirts at markets, or anything she could buy low and sell high. Exhausted and homesick, the final straw came when a large amount of her money was stolen, money she had borrowed from friends to buy stock to sell. Her mother was not well at the time and wanted Nga to come back to Hanoi. So, with little to show for her efforts Nga returned home in 1992. Through her late father's work colleagues she was able to get a job as a maid at the Post Office Guesthouse.

The Post Office Guesthouse was used to accommodate officials from provincial posts and telecommunications departments when they came to Hanoi on business. Sometimes there were foreign visitors staying at the Guesthouse and so Nga needed to learn English. She attended some night classes at first, but mostly she taught herself the basics. Then in 1993 until 1998 she went to evening classes at the Foreign Languages University and studied English there. Nga used the opportunity of having me, a native English speaker staying at the Guesthouse, to practice her skills. She was always testing out new words on me, the longer and more obscure the better. 'He is a punctilious man' she said about one director we both knew. 'The weather in Hanoi is capricious' she would observe. 'What's the longest English word you know?' she would ask, as she flipped through my dictionary.

At the end of 1996, the Post Office Guesthouse threw out all the beds and replaced them with desks. The Guesthouse was no more, as VNPT needed extra office space. It was more cost-effective to use the nearby mini-hotels that had mushroomed in recent times when provincial staff came to Hanoi on business. Nga remained on the staff of VNPT as a cleaner until she finally graduated from the Foreign Languages University in 1998 and was given an office job as a typist in the Administration Department of VNPT.

These days, Nga's economic life has improved. In 2004 she earns almost US$150 per month, five times what she earned eight years ago and enough to live on in Hanoi. She has enough to eat, can afford nice clothes and even fashionable hair colouring. She doesn't have a motorbike, not because she can't afford one but because she doesn't want one, preferring her bicycle for getting around. But her social life is severely lacking. Nga is not married at thirty-four and has no boyfriend. In Vietnam that is considered being 'on the shelf'. She says her life is boring and she feels old. Looking back Nga remembers the days of working at the Post Office Guesthouse as the happiest time of her life. Even though she worked hard and studied at the same time, she was meeting different people coming and going at the Guesthouse, going out with friends and colleagues and was looking forward to the future. Now, she works in a room with only one woman soon to retire and although she interacts with other staff nearby and at the canteen at lunchtime, it seems that after six years of working there it has become a humdrum existence. 'Money isn't the most important thing in life,' she says wistfully. 'I have to do something to change my life.'

Mrs Luu
shop owner

The first supermarket in Hanoi opened in 1995. Before that if foreigners needed toothpaste, washing powder, shampoo, breakfast cereals, chocolates, spreads and tinned foods, milk or even toilet paper they had little choice. They either brought supplies with them, went to Singapore on supermarket shopping excursions, or relied on a few small shops that kept an unreliable supply and an eclectic mix of imported goods. One such small shop was in Ngo Quyen Street not far from the Sofitel Metropole Hotel, a western oasis in the middle of Hanoi.

Once I had settled into my spartan room at the Post Office Guesthouse I decided to go exploring to find some basic supplies such as coffee, sugar, biscuits, maybe even some chocolate. Eventually I found Vinh's mother's shop. The shop was less than three metres wide and the same deep, with stock spilling out onto the street. It held a variety of goods ranging from Johnny Walker whisky, Coca-Cola (from China or Thailand), Danish biscuits, squashed and melted Mars Bars, New Zealand long-life milk, French butter, cigarettes, Lipton tea and tinned meats.

Sitting on a small stool ready to serve any customers was a young man who looked about fifteen but who was in fact about twenty-two years old. This was Vinh; anxious to practice his limited English so he could improve his business and always ready to help in any way. After I had purchased my instant coffee from him I went looking to buy an electric jug or kettle. When I couldn't find any, I went back to ask Vinh, and off he went on his motorbike to buy me one while I waited at his shop. And it was the same whenever I couldn't find something, Vinh would find it for me. Every time I passed his shop I would be invited to sit on a spare stool and have a drink and some conversation. If I was looking a bit tired, Vinh would give me a lift home on the back of his motorbike. If he were busy he would arrange for his brother-in-law to take me.

The shop belonged to Vinh's mother, Luu, and she was always supervising operations, from when it opened at 7 a.m. until it shut at about 10 p.m. or 11 p.m. seven days a week. Luu was born in 1939, the youngest of six children. Her family lived in Gia Lam, now a growing suburb of Hanoi, but then a rural area on the outskirts of the city. Her parents had a small piece of land where they grew food. Luu went to the village school until 1955 when she moved to Hanoi to live with her sister and her uncle's family in their house in Ngo Quyen Street. Her older sister had moved to Hanoi earlier and married a Vietnamese man of Chinese origin who became well known as a photographer and they had a photography shop in Hanoi. They had enough money to help Luu get started, with a small shop selling various goods, mainly groceries and clothes, when she came to live with them. Then, in 1959, Luu got married and her first son, Duc, was born a year later. After that she got a job in a state-owned food service company as a beverage maker and waitress, working there for twenty-five years until she was eligible for an early retirement. This job proved to be a considerable benefit to the family, not because of the wage that was low like most government jobs, but because she had better access to food and coupons during those difficult times of food shortages. Even then life was not easy, especially after her husband died suddenly one winter from complications from the flu aged only forty-eight years, leaving Luu and her three children to manage alone.

After she got married, Luu continued to live in the same house with her sister and her sister's husband and children. In 1979 when Vietnam and China were fighting, Luu's sister's husband, fearing trouble because of his Chinese ancestry, left Hanoi. He sailed from Hai Phong to Hong Kong, leaving his family behind because of the dangers of travelling by ship at that time. Once he reached Hong Kong he was planning to apply to go to Australia, but the British Government, aware of his reputation as a photographer, invited him to go to the UK and promised they would support his family to go there, too. But it wasn't until 1982 that his family was finally able to join him there.

With the sole use of the house in Ngo Quyen Street now that her sister and family had all gone, Luu decided in 1985, upon her retirement, to make use of the favourable location and started a small café. Then, with the introduction of the government's open door policy which encouraged private business and brought more foreigners to Vietnam, Luu realised that she had an ideal location to expand her business and it became a grocery and liquor store, supplying imported goods to visitors. By the time I came to know the family in 1994, the eldest son Duc was married with children of his own, but still lived and worked in his mother's shop. Her daughter was also married but she lived with her husband's family, and Vinh, the youngest son, also helped in the shop while he was studying at university.

The business must have been going well. In 1996 Duc decided he wanted to see something of the world now that Vietnam had begun to open up, and applied to the British Embassy for a visa to visit his aunt in England. To make the cost of the trip worthwhile, he wanted to stay a few months and see as much as he could of the west whose goods he had been selling for years. There was great excitement at the prospect of this trip. He was practising his English and preparing all the documents required, however, his application was rejected. He showed me the letter he received from the British Embassy, which stated that because it would take all his life-savings to pay for his trip, it was feared he would not come back to Vietnam and so a tourist visa would not be granted. Duc was devastated by the news. He had no wish to stay in England. His wife and children were in Hanoi and so was his business. All he wanted was to realise his dream of freedom and adventure before he got too old. He never seemed to recover from the disappointment of this refusal and aged quickly after that. He used his money to move with his wife and children to another house and opened his own grocery store, leaving more responsibility on his young brother Vinh to look after his mother's shop.

Vinh was also ambitious and wanted to travel abroad, but he adopted a different strategy. He decided he would have more chance if he enrolled in a course of study overseas and eventually found an Australian college that would accept him. In 2001, Vinh headed off to Australia, leaving his mother to live alone and his brother and sister to help her run the shop. Three years later he is still in Australia and has just had his visa extended another two years.

Over the years I had less and less need to buy from Vinh's shop. I lost the need for many imported goods, relying on local products that had increased in number and quality. Once the supermarkets opened it was more convenient to use them with their better range of goods. Vinh's mother's shop survives although I suspect it is not as lucrative as it was in the past when there was less competition. As the years pass, Luu is anxiously awaiting the return of her youngest son to take over the business, a task I suspect he is not at all keen to take on after living an independent life in Australia for so long.

Mrs Huong
market stall owner

Mrs Huong's is a great success story. These days she keeps her old stall in the well-known Hom Market on Hue Street, as well as two new trendy sales spaces in Hanoi's most modern plaza in Trang Tien Street right opposite Hoan Kiem Lake in the very heart of the city. But it hasn't been an easy road for her and the memory of some of the most difficult years still moves her to tears.

Huong was born in 1958, the youngest daughter of five children. Life was not easy for the family, surviving only on the small salary of her father who worked in a Government department under the Finance Ministry. During the time of the Vietnam War, Huong was sent to the rural areas to escape the bombing raids on Hanoi, but she managed to finish high school at eighteen years of age. Huong went on to study at the technical college of the State-owned electricity company, earning a third-level worker certificate after three years of study. She spent the next fifteen years working at the electricity company. Although there were many difficulties during the war years, Huong says that at least there was support from other countries to sustain the Vietnamese; but the years after the end of the war were the most difficult economically.

In 1987, Huong met Mr Kim at a friend's birthday party. He was thirteen years older and a school teacher from a rich family of traders. Once they married, Huong moved from her family's home to live in Mr Kim's house. In 1988 her son was born and in 1991 she had a daughter. During maternity leave with her first baby, Huong decided to open a small stall at the old Hom market to supplement her salary.

Although intending to do this only for six months, Huong managed to keep both the stall and her job going until the opportunity came for early retirement from the electricity company in 1991. This was during the period where the Government was offering voluntary early retirement packages with lump sum payments to reduce the number of workers in the inefficient state-owned enterprises.

1991 was a difficult year for Huong. She had retired from her government job, but after the birth of her daughter she divorced her husband. Now she had to be sure that she made a success of her market stall, since she received no financial support from her ex-husband. These days Huong says that she is good at selling because she was once very poor. She enjoys it, finds it easy and interesting and, given her success, is clearly very good at it. But success doesn't come easily. Even now, she starts her working day at 7 a.m., collects stock, works at Hom market until 5 p.m., goes home to cook dinner for the family, then goes to her shops at Trang Tien Plaza until closing at 10 p.m. She still isn't satisfied, wanting to grow her business even more.

In 2001, Huong's life became happier when she married again. Her new husband is an actor in the Army and is well known on Vietnamese television. Huong met him at a birthday party and fell in love with him when she heard him sing. These days she goes to watch him perform when she has any free time. Her happiness and success gave her more confidence to expand and so she decided to travel to Thailand and China to buy stock, without any previous experience or connections. Unable to speak Chinese or Thai, at first she hired an interpreter. Then, she decided she could do it herself using just her hands and a calculator to communicate.

Recently, there was a reunion for Huong's class at the electrical college after thirty years and Huong felt proud to realise that she and just three or four others have achieved such a level of success. She also knows that she is unlike most of the other stall-holders around her in the market, being much more ambitious and successful.

But the casual observer could easily miss the changes that have occurred in Huong's life. Ten years ago I would sometimes go and sit in Huong's claustrophobic cubicle on a tiny stool a few inches off the ground and try to communicate with her with a few words of Vietnamese and lots of hand and facial gestures. And that's still where I meet her. We sit on the same plastic stools. The difference is that she looks happier, wears more expensive clothes and makeup and has a manager to look after her other shops located in luxurious air-conditioned surroundings. These shops cost almost as much to rent a month, as she would once have earned in ten years working at the electricity company.

Mr Hanh
fortune teller

Mr Hanh was the first fortune teller I ever visited. On that first visit, my friend Mrs Thanh and I went by motorbike taxi to his house, almost ten kilometres from the centre of Hanoi. We sat in his small bare cement room, furnished with a wooden bed, small low desk, a few chairs and a small altar on a high shelf. We shuffled cards and selected rods, shook coins and took notes as he told us our fortunes.

I found Mr Hanh's pronouncements frighteningly accurate at times; he could describe my character and give a reasonable account of past events. But when he was able to describe my eldest son's front teeth and accurately predict, to the week, the payment of a large sum of money to me I started to think this man had special powers. I couldn't fathom how he could know such things, since it didn't fit with any belief system I had. I was prepared to suspend my judgement and revisited him a few times over the years with various interpreters to help me. Now, almost ten years after my first visit I was back there again, only this time I was more interested in what I could learn about Mr Hanh's past than in my future.

Very little had changed in his physical surroundings in ten years. The room was still austere, with the same furniture, peeling paint on the walls and no floor covering. He still had his same dusty reference materials neatly piled by his side, the same diagrams under the glass of his desk top, only now he needed his glasses to read them. I had expected him to be reluctant to talk about his fortune telling, first because the Vietnamese Government actively disapproves of superstitious practices and secondly because I thought he would want to maintain an air of mystery or secrecy about his craft. However, I was wrong on both counts.

Hanh was born in 1944. Like me he is a Monkey, according to the Vietnamese lunar calendar. His mother died when he was eighteen years old but his father is still going strong at eighty-three. Hanh was the eldest child and only son, having two younger sisters.

He joined the Army when he was nineteen years old and studied medicine, becoming a medical worker (in Vietnam this position is ranked below a doctor but above a nurse) for high-ranking Army officers until he took an early retirement at the age of forty-four.

While he was studying medicine he had the opportunity to read a lot of books on a wide variety of topics including eastern medicine and fortune telling. His interest and curiosity grew over the years and he began to talk to others who had skills and knowledge about fortune telling, especially some old men. When he first started to practise his craft his successful predictions and people's belief in him encouraged him to study more and since his job was to provide medical service only to high-ranking officers, he had a lot of free time to do this.

Hanh and his wife have lived in this simple house since 1979 and raised their four children there. Times were hard during and just after the war and like almost everyone in Vietnam, they were poor and focused on survival. Now, all three daughters have jobs and their youngest son is studying at an IT college.

If it's hard to be a prophet in one's own country, it is almost impossible to be one in one's own family, it seems. His children tend not to ask for his help, but sometimes he pro-actively gives them advice. Certainly there has been no question of any of them taking on this work. According to Hanh, it is something you have to want to do and so far there is no-one for him to hand his knowledge to. As far as worrying about the Government, Hanh says that he gives suggestions about when and what to be careful of. He says he is not encouraging people to do special practices like making offerings and prayers. Certainly he doesn't derive much material benefit from his services, charging only a minimal amount for each consultation and living on his retirement pension. According to Hanh, fortune telling is mainly a science with methodologies and knowledge tested and proven over the centuries. He does admit there is some art to it and that it utilises his special Monkey sixth sense. 'However,' he mused as I was about to leave, 'it is not always easy if you see too much. Maybe life would be easier if I had seen and understood less.'

Mrs Phuong
tea lady

All over Vietnam there are women, mostly old, who sit on the street corners or in small alleyways on stools behind low tables dispensing small cups of tea costing just a few cents. Some stay at their post all day and part of the night, others focus just on peak periods. Mrs Phuong selected the busy, noisy corner of Nguyen Du and Hue streets for her tea stand and operates there every day from 5 p.m. until 9.30 p.m. in wintertime and until about 11 p.m. in summer..

I don't particularly like the green tea of North Vietnam, although over the years I have had to drink gallons of it conforming to protocol in business and social meetings, so I had never bought tea from Mrs Phuong. However, on my way to Mrs Noodles, chicken soup shop across the road, or to Mr Suu's fried beef noodles stand, I would regularly pass by her tea stall and we would nod and smile at each other. There was something about the sparkle in her eyes, the lively animation of her face that made me wonder about her life. When I returned to Hanoi after an absence of eighteen months, Mrs.Phuong greeted me enthusiastically when I walked by; she clearly missed seeing me and registered my return. She invited me to have a cup of tea with her. This was my chance to hear her story.

Born in Hanoi in 1946, Phuong loved the theatre, especially *cai luong* or reformed opera—a little like traditional Chinese opera. There was a *cai luong* theatre group near her house and she would go there as often as possible, learning many of the songs by heart. When she was eighteen years old she went for an audition to join the group and because she was already so familiar with their repertoire and could perform the songs well, she was accepted. After two years of training she began to perform for the Army, sometimes in Hanoi, but also travelling all over the north of Vietnam to entertain soldiers during the war, from about 1966 to 1969.

However, once Phuong met her future husband her performing days were over. If they were to be married, he said, she would have to quit the troupe. Since she was one of their best performers they were sorry to lose her, but they couldn't persuade her husband to change his mind and so Phuong gave up the bright lights to become a wife and to work in a machine factory in Hanoi.

Phuong had one very close call when she was on tour entertaining the soldiers. During a bombing attack by the Americans she was taking cover in one bomb shelter when, for some reason, she moved to a shelter nearby. Shortly after, the shelter she had left was destroyed by a direct hit. Working in Hanoi in those days was not much safer. One evening, only minutes after all the workers had left the factory following a meeting, it too was bombed. The following morning the workers couldn't believe their eyes or their luck when they saw their destroyed factory. Phuong's third bomb incident occurred when the French Embassy in Hanoi was bombed. Her house backed onto that building and in the resulting fire she lost all the photos from her performing career.

The Government of Vietnam presented Phuong with an award for service during the war. In 1990 she took early retirement from the machine factory and began her tea stall. She has two sons and two daughters, three of them with jobs and the youngest still studying at the National Economics University. They all tell her she has no need to sell cups of tea these days as they earn enough to support the family, but she enjoys it. Even on cold and wet wintry nights she is happy to be there, rugged up in a parka with the hood tightly drawn around her tiny face that once was known for its white skin and rosy cheeks. In the warmer weather she wears a small scarf tied around her hair. 'Like the little Dutch girl on the Dutch Jug milk cartons,' she says. During the day she looks after her grandchildren, but the evening is her time. And I suspect from the chatter and laughter around her stall that for those hours she is back in her element as an entertainer.

Not all the old familiar faces were still around when I returned to Hanoi. Mrs Noodles had apparently moved to Ho Chi Minh City a couple of years ago to start a business there, although someone thought that she and her husband had divorced and only he went to Ho Chi Minh City. Whatever the story, her well-known chicken noodle soup shop remains, but only a shadow of its former self, looking somewhat run-down. No doubt the situation wasn't helped by the chicken flu epidemic that saw all chicken products abandoned for some months. I miss her and her pretty little daughter. The motorbike washers in Tran Quoc Toan Street whose sound of running water would soothe me on those blistering, still summer days were long gone, along with the barber who had his chair and mirror under a nearby tree. Three of the houses I once lived in have been converted to commercial ventures, one a karaoke bar, one a café and another near the cathedral is now a silk shop.

Of course, not all the lives that intersected with mine originated on the streets. Like the finest embroidery found here, the life of Hanoi is closely stitched together. There are many threads to choose from should you desire and when one thread ends there are many more to pick up and follow through the design.

Mrs Nga
MBA

My friend Mrs Nga serves as an example of the many Vietnamese who never stop striving to better themselves intellectually and materially and who do everything they can to improve their children's life chances. Nga's father was born in Nghe An province, the place where Ho Chi Minh was born. He joined the Communist revolution in 1945 and in 1951 he was sent to join the Army and fought against the French in Dien Bien Phu. Finally he returned to Hanoi to settle down with the wife he had hardly seen during those eight years. After eleven years of marriage their first daughter was born in 1959. Nga was born in 1961 and they had another daughter in 1963. Finally in 1971 they had twin girls, called Hong and Ha, meaning 'flooded Red River' because they were born during the biggest flood Hanoi had experienced.

When she was only sixteen, Nga won a scholarship to study in Ukraine. First she had to study Russian language for six months in

Hanoi. Then she studied for her degree in semiconductors and micro-electronics (taught in Russian language) at the Technical University of Lvov from 1978 to 1983. During those five years, Nga was unable to afford to return to Vietnam but she tried to satisfy her curiosity about the world around her. She had to earn money to be able to pay for any travel and so she tried her hand at anything that was available. She worked in factories or fields in neighbouring Eastern European countries during her university summer vacations. She remembers ruining some of the products at a ball-bearing factory and a furniture factory when she was working on a production line because she was more interested in reading her book than taking care with her job. After a stint of harvesting potatoes and tomatoes in Eastern Germany, she came back to university almost unrecognisable; she recalls being fat from eating potatoes, with dark skin from working outside.

When she finished her degree she returned to Hanoi and began work at the National Research Institute for Natural Sciences. Because there was no money to undertake practical experimentation in the areas the Institute was interested in, such as electronics, wind power and robotics, activities were mainly confined to reading and seminars. In 1986 she married and had a daughter. In 1988 she was among the few selected to go to Moscow to work as an interpreter in training programs on economic management for Government officials, leaving behind her small child for ten months.

In 1991 she met a friend in Hanoi who told her about an Australian company that needed an English speaker and someone with computer skills. Nga was skilled at computing and had even run some computing classes. When she first returned to Hanoi, she began to study English for fun, since it was a bit of a fashion in Hanoi at the time. However, she says she didn't get much practice in speaking and listening to English and she often didn't know what was said to her in those early days. Nevertheless, she got the job. Over the years the company itself changed but Nga remained in charge of managing operations.

I first met Nga in 1994 when I became friendly with her Australian boss and his wife. In 1997, the same year that she had her second child, the company she was working for agreed to sponsor her studies in a Henley MBA distance-learning program and, as I was tutoring some subjects in this program, I got to know her even better. Henley College is among the top twenty business schools in Europe and so the standard required is high. Yet despite working in her third language (English) and still holding a responsible job and looking after her extended family, including elderly parents and a small son, she managed to pass her course and study some French language for relaxation. In 2003, Nga went to Henley College in the UK to receive her MBA degree at the graduation ceremony, and her husband, who works for the Vietnam airport administration, and her daughter, who had just won a part-scholarship to attend a private high school in the UK, were able to go too.

Nga's work and studies have provided her with a number of opportunities to live and travel abroad, but she is a true Hanoian, and even though she still enjoys travel, Hanoi is where she wants to live permanently. She also wants her daughter to have the same opportunity as she did, of living and studying abroad, to build her independence and confidence. Nga expects that when her daughter completes her studies at high school and then university, she too will come back from England and settle in Hanoi.

Nga's story is not unique in this amazing country. Every foreigner who comes to work in Vietnam will have collected many such stories that leave us in awe of the talent and the sacrifice that generations of Vietnamese have made not only in the battle for independence and peace, but in leaving behind their families for years, enduring difficult conditions overseas, struggling with their studies in their second or third language, all in the hope of improving themselves and giving their children a better life.

Mr Loc
drum teacher

Living alone in Hanoi for a long time without the easy distractions of television, movies or theatre and without family and long-time friends around, or familiar recreational activities, I decided I needed to create non-work outlets and pastimes. I preferred activities that led me into Vietnamese life and experiences, rather than hanging around some café or bar frequented by foreigners. I had already had ballroom dancing lessons, singing lessons and ping-pong lessons, where a very tolerant old teacher allowed me to play in high heels because I didn't own a pair of sneakers. Wondering what to do next, I remembered a teenage dream I had to play drums. I could still recall the drummer at Barry Navin's twenty-first birthday party in Griffith, in country NSW, allowing me to have a try on his drums thirty years earlier. I mentioned the idea to Mr. Dzung, my dancing teacher, who immediately said he would introduce me to a teacher he knew. That's how I came to meet Mr Loc.

A tiny energetic man in his forties, Loc lived with his family in a small dilapidated set of rooms on a main street in the centre of Hanoi. His room was just wide enough at the front to fit an old drum kit in front of a window that had a metal grille and no glass and looked directly onto the footpath. The room widened at the back to where a wooden ladder led to sleeping quarters for the family. This room was like a cement cave, with no decoration, a few rough wooden planks for shelves, some small, low stools, a set of coat hooks on the wall and space for his old battered bicycle. Mr Loc couldn't speak English but he was undaunted by the prospect of teaching an old Australian woman who had only a smattering of Vietnamese and we settled on Sunday mornings as the time for my lessons.

For US$50, I could buy a drum kit that included cymbal, hi-hat, toms, side drum, and a snare. It was made in Vietnam and sounded rather tinny, with a pedal that squeaked, but certainly it was good enough for my needs. At first, I worried about making too much noise and felt self-conscious about practising, until I asked a friend to bang on the drums while I stood outside to hear how it sounded. I quickly realised that my addition to the cacophony of noises in the street was minimal.

I really enjoyed my lessons every Sunday morning with Mr Loc. They were rather relaxed affairs with me plodding away practising my cha-cha or rhumba rhythm while Mr Loc kept time for me as he smoked a cigarette or chatted with a friend who might have dropped in. Neighbourhood kids would poke their faces through the grille at the front window to stare at the foreigner playing drums. Sometimes Mr Loc would make me dance the rhythms. Other times I had to practice my timing exercises on a piece of wood. He had no music or books to teach from. We got by with him just writing the symbols in a notebook for me to follow. Of course, I never became much of a drummer, but I did find it good therapy. It allowed me to participate in making music, it was good exercise and was a great way to let off steam after a frustrating day at work.

In fact, Mr Loc wasn't much of a drummer either, if truth be told. He was more of an eccentric philosopher. On those occasions where he had a visitor or another student who could speak English, he would speak deeply about his theories of dance and music. I enjoyed seeing how the small amount of money I paid him each week made a visible difference to his life. Each week there would be another improvement to the room, a coat of paint on the walls, a mirror, new stools, a brighter light—small things that he could now afford. And I was able to introduce him to another foreigner, a young Danish boy who wanted lessons.

I eventually reached a point where I didn't think there was much more I could learn from Mr Loc. I became busy with other things and slowly my interest in drumming waned. Before I went back to Australia I sold my drums. I tried an evening class of African drumming in Sydney for a while, but it wasn't the same. When I returned to Hanoi I called in to say hello to Mr Loc one afternoon.

According to a new sign outside his room, he had now branched out to teach dancing. The day I happened by he had two couples squeezed into his tiny space, teaching them the cha-cha. Nevertheless he insisted I come in with my friend for a chat. He excitedly retrieved a photo of me taken with my drums that he had kept hanging on the wall and told everyone how I had been his student. Then he became very serious and asked my friend to tell me that he was very grateful to me for two reasons. He explained that in the past he had only taught drumming to young men and boys. But after people had seen me coming for lessons every Sunday, he had acquired a number of old women students! I thought this was hysterical and could imagine baffled anthropologists in years to come pondering this blip in the society, wondering why drumming suddenly became fashionable for middle-aged Hanoian women in the last decade of the twentieth century. Then to top off my visit, he went on to explain that he had recently been asked to teach some disabled children and after his experience with me he understood the teaching techniques to do that!

Over the years I have met many Vietnamese, either teaching them or teaching with them, interviewing them for jobs, working with them or just playing with them. I am in awe of the intellectual capacity of so many of them, and their drive and tenacity, often under conditions of extreme hardship. I have also seen huge fortunes made in the last ten years. The door to this country only needed to be opened a crack to get the entrepreneurs off and running. From a few tiny shops, the ancient silk street has grown to a huge number of extremely lucrative businesses selling locally and exporting silk and embroidered products. Others who were fortunate enough to have land were able to take advantage of the influx of foreigners working here and build houses for them to rent at exorbitant prices initially when supply was low and demand high, or to build mini-hotels for the tourists. Tour companies are another success story. There was some luck involved in these big successes and they often had some advantage, either land, connections or education. But it also required a leap of imagination, a change in thinking and a lot of hard work to imagine and then start to create a new and very different world from the one that the people of Vietnam had experienced for generations.

I have one more story I want to tell. The story of Mr Thac is an interesting one, especially because it dispels the notion that foreigners are the only ones able and willing to give aid to Vietnamese.

Mr Thac
school founder

Mr Thac was born in 1938. That makes him a Tiger according to the Vietnamese calendar; a forest tiger he told me, laughing at the idea. When I checked the characteristics of the Tiger personality I too smiled. Mr Thac seemed far too mild-mannered to ever be described as passionate and angry, clawing those who disobey him. But I soon found out that behind that slight exterior and those twinkling eyes he did indeed hide the heart of a Tiger—a person described as ready to 'invest in a new undertaking without hesitation, confident in his luck and intuition ... In time becoming a magnificent hero who lights up the world.'

By the time he had reached his early thirties Mr Thac was already a bit of a hero. After studying electronics at the Hanoi University of Technology he was sent to Moscow for two years to work with radar experts. Armed with this new knowledge and an inventive mind, Thac returned to Hanoi to improve the city's radar defences against the American B52 bombers during the Vietnam War, winning praise for his efforts. At the end of the war in 1975, he left his position as Army Captain and went to work at the Industry Technology Research Institute in Hanoi where he stayed until 1993. He took an early retirement at age fifty-five.

All his life Thac had been interested in inventing new products and processes. His son Thanh remembers their small family home always cluttered with his father's equipment and experiments when he was growing up. During the difficult days after the war, when almost everyone was poor and everything scarce, the whole family was involved in various projects, trying to supplement Thac's meagre government salary. 'Even my mother can repair electrical equipment,' says Thanh proudly. 'I built my own set of speakers as a teenager.'

In addition to repairing electronic equipment, Thac also developed an electricity surge stabiliser, a popular product during times of poor power generation, and his son would go out selling them. He also developed ways of reducing the amount of material required to produce items such as electric fans without compromising performance, thereby saving manufacturing costs. Well ahead of his time, Thac developed a cleaning process using ultrasound that he published in scientific journals. His idea was for doctors to use it to thoroughly clean their hands, removing all traces of dirt even from under their fingernails. But no-one had the capital or was interested in exploiting his ideas in a big way at that time. 'My father thinks that if he had been born somewhere like America, he would have become rich and famous,' says his son.

Retirement for Thac didn't mean doing nothing or wasting time on his own pleasure. He began teaching at a Government vocational school and wrote an electronics training book. The pay for this work was very small, maybe enough to buy a bowl of noodle soup each day and that's all. So he also started holding small classes in electronics in his home for private students. In 2000, when he was sixty-two, he sold his own house to rent some buildings, equip the classrooms, pay for advertising and for all the various government charges, and began the Thang Long Vocational School in Dong Da District in Hanoi. 'I was worried it was too hard for him and he faced many difficulties at first,' says his son. 'I wanted him to invest in property to ensure his comfort in his old age, but my father wanted to do something socially useful and use his knowledge to help others, especially disadvantaged students.'

I had come to know Mr Thac's son, Thanh, through mutual friends and it was only by accident that one day the conversation turned to his father and his amazing achievement. At first I was expecting to be told that Mr Thac had taught maybe a few dozen students, so I was amazed to learn that by the end of 2003, seven hundred students had passed through his school. Almost all of them found work straight away. Clearly this was not an old man pottering about and filling in time during his dotage and I was keen to meet him and see for myself.

By this time the number of teachers employed at the school had grown to fifteen and there were courses in repairing motorbikes, electronic equipment such as televisions, video players, CD players, telephones, sewing machines and tailoring. Not content to rest on his laurels, Mr Thac is planning to expand the school to a second campus that will run courses in car mechanics, photocopy machine repairs, industrial equipment repairs and cookery. The school also provides very cheap, basic hostel accommodation for students living away from home to ensure they have a safe and secure environment.

It is not an easy balancing act for Thac. He wants to attract and keep good teachers and so he must pay them well, he wants class sizes kept small to ensure the transfer of practical skills, but he also wants fees that are affordable for ordinary students and provide scholarships for poor and disadvantaged students. Recently, an Australian entrepreneur and philanthropist, Colin Macfarlane, has provided a helping hand to Thac in the form of some equipment for the school and scholarships for ethnic minorities and disadvantaged students, especially those still suffering as a result of the war. So far the results have been gratifying.

Mr Thac is understandably proud of his success stories, stories of changed lives and new opportunities that break the cycle of poverty. Miss Banh is a thirty-year-old Thai ethnic from Lai Chau, a province in the far north-west of Vietnam bordering China and Laos. Married with a daughter, Banh grew rice with the rest of her village until a scholarship from Colin changed her life. She left her family and came to Hanoi for six months to study tailoring at the school. On completion of the course she returned home, and with the support of her extended family, opened a tailoring shop at the front of her brother-in-law's house in Dien Bien Phu. She still works hard, but in a more pleasant environment than the rice fields, and earns more.

'My father keeps getting younger and younger and he is always smiling these days,' says his son. 'He is more open to new ideas and keeps learning new things. Now he carries a mobile phone. He is always busy. I really respect him because I don't think I could be like him when I am old.' If you ask Thac about his own money that he has invested he just laughs and says, 'You can't take it to the heavens when you die, but it can help poor students.' With the rising cost of rent and overheads, Thac is worried that he will not be able expand enough to meet the enormous demand for training unless he gets more sponsorship. But this tiger isn't letting go. A decade after retiring Thac is only getting started.

Jimmy's Story:
Know One Teach One

Jimmy is a big bear of a man with a heart to match. A heart so big that there is room in it for hundreds of Vietnam's street kids, all of them wrapped up securely in the warmth of his love. Jimmy wasn't a street kid himself, although he might have been one if not for the strength and determination of his mother who inspires and supports him still. But a walk around Saigon late one night changed Jimmy's life, and at twenty-four years of age he found what he believes is his purpose in life.

To be born in Saigon (now Ho Chi Minh City) in 1972 when the Vietnam War was still being fiercely fought was not the best start to life. However, Jimmy's family managed to flee Vietnam in 1974 and spent three years in Singapore and another three years in Saudi Arabia before ending up in Australia when Jimmy was eight years old.

Even before these adventures his parents' story was like the plot of a soap opera. Jimmy's mother was an only child whose mother left her when she was born and whose father died when she was thirteen years old, leaving her to fend for herself from that time onward. She was a simple country girl, illiterate and unskilled, who survived by doing many different jobs and eventually made her way to Saigon. She had four children before meeting Jimmy's father, a Korean soldier who was serving eight years in Vietnam. According to Jimmy, his father was a super-intelligent man who worked as an architect and could speak three languages. However, he was also a dreamer; always chasing rainbows looking for that elusive pot of gold and neglecting his responsibilities to his family. It was Jimmy's mother who held the family together and supported them. She fought to get all her children out of Saigon to Singapore and then to Saudi Arabia. It was her effort, baking bread and donuts that made them a comfortable living in Saudi Arabia so that they could afford a four-storey house and a chauffeur to take young Jimmy to school. After leaving her husband in Saudi Arabia, it was Jimmy's mother who single-handedly raised and supported her children in Australia, working day and night.

'Everything was for us, her children,' says Jimmy about his mother. 'Now, when I think about it, I believe that my mother was a western woman trapped in an Asian culture. She has such a strong character and speaks her mind—not always appreciated by Asian men!' By the time they were living in Saudi Arabia, Jimmy's parents had drifted further apart. His father had accumulated debts, his schemes had run aground and he had problems getting a visa for Australia. He stayed behind, telling Jimmy at the airport, 'Take care of your mother. I'll see you soon.' This was another broken promise and Jimmy grew up in Australia without seeing his father again.

But there was still a surprise in store for Jimmy. When he turned twenty-one he wanted to put the past to rest and put aside the anger he had felt as an adolescent towards his absent father. It took six months to find his father, surprisingly still living in Saudi Arabia after all those years. There were phone calls and letters exchanged over the following months; then a revelation that Jimmy had a half-brother from his father's first marriage who was now in his thirties and living in Korea. 'Give him an opportunity to be a good brother,' his father told Jimmy. To Jimmy's mother, in what was to be their final telephone conversation, he said, 'Anything I need to tell my son I have said already.' Not long after that, they received a call from a voice that they didn't recognise. It was Jimmy's half-brother in Korea calling to say, in the only English words he knew, 'Our father just died.' He had died alone in a small room in Saudi Arabia with almost no furniture and in debt. The Saudi Government had taken his passport because of his debts and it took six weeks to clear up matters to have his body released for burial in Korea. With his mother and sister, Jimmy went to the funeral where he finally laid to rest the father he hardly knew, and gained a half-brother with whom he felt bonded now, despite not sharing a language.

On leaving Saudi Arabia, Jimmy's mother had the choice of going to Australia or the United States. Her eldest daughter had married an American diplomat in Saudi and had moved to the United States. Her eldest son had already gone to Australia as a refugee after leaving Singapore and was also able to sponsor the rest of the family. Jimmy's mother decided that her son needed her more than her daughter at that time and so Australia was chosen for their new home.

This uneducated woman, who had a limited English vocabulary that she learnt from her Korean husband, still managed to raise and educate her children and prosper in a new country, while her educated, polyglot husband died alone and in poverty. Life was not easy, and the whole family slept in one room when they first arrived. As they earned money, they gradually bought furniture and pots and pans. At first Jimmy's mother did sewing at home, working till after midnight. After four years they opened a grocery store, and later a butcher's shop, as well as operated various stalls at weekend markets—anything to ensure the family prospered.

Jimmy attended Catholic schools in Sydney, Australia until he decided to leave in Year 11. After that he worked at various jobs in video stores and a caravan park. As soon as he got his provisional driver's licence he bought a cheap car with his savings and headed for Melbourne to visit his married sister. He ended up selling vacuum cleaners for two years, gaining swift promotion in the company. But something was missing for Jimmy, so he headed back to Sydney for a while, worked some more and decided to go to TAFE in Canberra, staying with his brother while he studied for his Higher School Certificate. 'It did three things; it gave me a sense of achievement; made Mum happy; and proved I could do it.'

At the end of his studies he went back to Sydney, and worked in a sandwich bar in Kings Cross. He saved enough money to visit his sister in the US and also went to Japan. He had visited Vietnam once with his mother when he was still at school, but this was his first experience of travelling abroad alone and he discovered a passion for travel, deciding that travel and tourism was the career he wanted to pursue. Once he got back from his trip he enrolled in a well-known private travel and tourism college where, after studying for a year and gaining his certificate, got himself a job with Travel Indochine.

1996 was a life-changing year for twenty-four-year old Jimmy. He was sent by Travel Indochine to Vietnam on a familiarisation tour when late one night, feeling bored, he went for a walk. For the first time he found himself amongst the street kids of Saigon. 'I spent the next two weeks with these kids, talking to them and trying to find them somewhere to sleep and to wash. I sat with them and saw the kid in them even though they tried so hard to be like adults. I saw the harshness of their lives.' Jimmy made the decision that he had to find a way of going back to Vietnam to help Vietnamese kids. 'I remember one day being greeted by four kids selling a coconut, and the coconut they were carrying weighed more than they did. I noticed how dirty they were. But they still had these remarkable radiant smiles. They captured my heart more than they could imagine.'

When Jimmy returned to Australia, he approached his company with the idea of being based in Vietnam as a tour leader. When they refused on the grounds that he didn't have enough knowledge of Vietnam, Jimmy left and found a job with Intrepid Travel who were prepared to send him to Vietnam. Jimmy had found his way back.

'Looking back now I don't know how I made it. I couldn't speak Vietnamese. My mother was scared for me. Vietnam for her was still a place about communism and police taking people away.' Jimmy managed to reassure his mother, telling her he would only stay a maximum of two years. That was more than seven years ago.

All his life, the happiness of others has been important to Jimmy. Although no saint as a kid, Jimmy always volunteered to work at the school canteen or as an altar boy; he enjoyed helping others. Along with his mother's strength and humanitarian values Jimmy also inherited a bit of the dreamer from his father; only his dream was to make a difference in the world. His search was for a sense of fulfilment and a pot filled with purpose rather than gold.

'If we can't look after our children, what else can we do right?' says Jimmy quietly. 'Children are our future.' Many people speak words like these, but few go as far as Jimmy in taking action. When he arrived back in Vietnam in 1996, Jimmy began a remarkable journey. 'I rediscovered my roots in Vietnam and at the same time I was taught the most valuable lesson of all: compassion.'

Based in Ho Chi Minh City for Intrepid Travel, Jimmy spent the next three years travelling in Vietnam, guiding tourists and living out of a suitcase. He found streets kids everywhere he went. Whenever he would go to the central Saigon area, street kids would gather around him. 'I understand now it was because they saw me as a big fat turkey and thought they should take the opportunity to get what they could. Tell me a sob story and out would come my wallet. Everything I ever had I gave them. Initially, I just wanted to find them somewhere to live and send them to learn some English. I thought at the time I was doing the right thing, but ended up living like them, just for today without thinking of tomorrow. I didn't have a sustainable plan.'

During those three years Jimmy learned a lot about Vietnam, the language, the culture and especially about street kids. As he criss-crossed the country he regularly checked on kids he had come to know in Hanoi, Hue, Hoi An, Nha Trang, Can Tho, outlaying about US$600 per month on their support. When the tourists were tucked safely in their beds, Jimmy was out with the kids on the streets, in the rubbish dumps and gutters trying to help. He saw these kids waiting for hours for tourists to come out of a restaurant on the promise of a 'maybe'. Maybe they would buy a postcard or maybe have a shoeshine. How could he save them all? He knew that what he was doing was not sustainable, yet how could he stop when they clearly needed help?

One day, something remarkable happened that changed things. It was as if a door opened and he was let inside. Nine street kids in Hanoi took him aside and told him that now they trusted him. But, wise beyond their years, they warned him that if he continued looking after them they wouldn't be able to look after themselves. All of them were getting older and not getting anywhere. They were only thirteen or fourteen when they first met Jimmy, but now they were sixteen and seventeen. 'We're going to need jobs,' they told him, 'proper jobs, not selling postcards and cleaning shoes.'

Jimmy had not much money and few skills, but he knew a bit about tourism and hospitality. He had worked in the school canteen, at RSL clubs, McDonald's and sandwich bars. He knew about fast food and how to make a milkshake. In 1999, with nothing but heart he took his own savings, borrowed from his mother, reduced his job to half-time and opened a sandwich shop with his nine Hanoi street kids. He lived with them and worked with them. He taught them about personal hygiene, working hygiene, about making sandwiches and drinks. They painted the shop together; they shared their food and their hopes.

One day one of the kids got really sick and Jimmy took him to the hospital. When he recovered, the kid looked him squarely in the eye and asked, 'What do you want from all this, Jimmy? Why are you so good to all of us?' Jimmy couldn't answer him at the time. He only knew that he was following his heart. But two months later he had an answer to give this kid and all the others that followed. 'You're right,' he told him, 'I do want something from you. I want you to become the best person you can be. And once you have found your life and security and happiness and can look after yourself and your family, then I want you to help someone else.'

Jimmy's philosophy is as simple and as profound as that. He believes that if you just help one person achieve his or her potential then you have done your bit for society. And from that the name KOTO was born—if you Know One you can Teach One. KOTO became the name of the hospitality training centre for street kids and the restaurant they run.

Although Jimmy grew up a Catholic he describes himself these days as a non-practising Christian who believes in holistic love. 'You can't just give these kids a vocational skill and nothing else. You have to look after their health, financial security, personal development, communication skills, knowledge, values and understanding. I also wanted my kids never to have to depend on anybody except themselves. I wanted to create a sense of family for them. I want them to feel part of a huge, wonderful, loving and dedicated family that stands behind them no matter where they are. I want them to always be completely confident that even if they fall it's okay and the family will always stand behind them.'

If you walk into KOTO today, that's exactly what you will feel. Somehow it feels like walking into a big soft warm mass of love. Every kid exudes an air of quiet confidence and a sense of wellbeing; they seem full of happiness and are well loved. These days, they are all squeaky-clean and professional in their work but they still have the radiant smiles that first captivated Jimmy and they still have much of the child inside that he saw. 'Those kids that saw me as just a big fat turkey underestimated me,' Jimmy laughs. 'I didn't come to Vietnam for the short-term. I came here to see how I could help. It's been a steep learning curve.'

After a year of operation, Jimmy's sandwich shop needed to expand and make more money if he was serious about starting a training centre. Jimmy believed in his kids, but at that time no-one else did. The kids believed in Jimmy and he couldn't let them down, so he went back to his mother for another loan. Jimmy credits living in Australia for developing his humanitarian attitude, but his inspiration comes from his mother and what he refers to as her 'simple honesty'. By lending him more money, 'my mother gave a kick-start to building my dream. Now I can kick-start one hundred lives; change their lives, help their families, break the cycle of poverty.'

Now KOTO is a fully licensed not-for-profit organisation registered with the Department of Planning and Investment under Hanoi's People's Committee and the Government of Vietnam's Department of Labour, Invalids and Social Affairs. The eighty-seat KOTO restaurant moved to its current site in September 2000 and was officially opened by the Australian Ambassador in Vietnam at the time, Michael Mann.

Bill Clinton, when he was US President, visited KOTO Restaurant with his wife and daughter in November 2000 after they had been to see the Temple of Literature across the road. The KOTO training centre opened in July 2001. Its training program these days runs for eighteen months. During this time trainees learn either cookery or bar and service skills and they all take part in English language classes that are tailored especially for the hospitality industry, as well as life skills activities. They also have the opportunity to apply their newly acquired talent in the KOTO restaurant. In March 2002, the first ever graduates of KOTO received their certificate in an emotional and heart-warming ceremony.

Such a factual description of the genesis of KOTO as it is today tells nothing of the struggle and sacrifice involved. They had to open and close five times before being allowed to operate. Jimmy was stretched to the limit. 'I was fatigued mentally, emotionally, physically but I couldn't just say: "I'm tired", when these kids were depending on me.' Sometimes he ran out of money. He had given up even his part-time job in travel to devote himself to KOTO full-time, with no pay. He collapsed three times. Jimmy has no time for a personal life outside of KOTO. And he still has to pay back his loans to his mother. Yet, he can still say, 'I love my job so much that I don't consider it work. I have found my purpose.'

According to official estimates, there are 19,000 children trying to survive on the streets of Hanoi but it could easily be double that number. When these numbers get so large we stop seeing individuals, and instead feel swamped by the 'problem'. But in fact, each of the 19,000 kids trying to survive on the streets of Hanoi is an individual with a story to tell and it is often a heart-wrenching story. Here are just four of them, all with happy endings thanks to a remarkable young man called Jimmy.

Hue's Story

In Vietnam the life of a buffalo is a hard one, always working and pulling a heavy load. This is also believed to be the destiny of those born in the Year of the Buffalo. That's when Hue was born, in 1985 in Hang Yen province. Her parents are rice farmers and she has two younger brothers. Hue spent nine years at school from 1990 to 1998 where she was a good student, best at English and French. But, when she was about to turn fourteen, her father became very ill and couldn't work, leaving the family in trouble. Hue felt she had no choice but to try her luck at finding work in Hanoi. Her mother tried to stop her and the memory of that time saddens her. She says simply, 'How could we live?'

Hue went to Hanoi all alone by bus. She tried to find a cousin who had already come to Hanoi to try her luck. Scared and lonely, she walked around the city for eleven days before finding a job washing dishes in one of the many street eateries. Her working day started at 7 a.m. and ended at 8 p.m. or 9 p.m. She was paid enough to live but not enough to send home, so she had to find another job. She tried selling vegetables, selling hats and finally selling postcards to tourists outside a well-known café near the Catholic cathedral in the centre of Hanoi. Selling postcards is a hard life; lots of kids try to eke out a living this way and so it is very competitive. When the weather is bad or there are no tourists in town it is hard to make any money at all; then there are the police to worry about, the drug addicts who sometimes try to steal the slim earnings and the tourists who are rude and abusive. Some of the foreigners were kind. One woman, a journalist working in Hanoi, paid for some English lessons for her. 'She was a very lovely lady and a second mum of mine, but then she left Vietnam.'

Hue sold postcards for more than two years, starting at 7 a.m. or 8 a.m. every day and going home to a small shared room at about 6 p.m. or 7 p.m. Then she met Jimmy which she says was the luckiest day of her life. 'I did not believe it, couldn't imagine it' when Jimmy explained to her about KOTO. 'I filled in the application form and then had to wait months for the next training course to start. I continued selling postcards but kept in close contact with Jimmy while I was waiting.'

The 'Monkey' statues at the Muong Thanh Hotel in Dien Bien Phu.

Mr Hieu, bicycle tyre repairman, Summer 1994.

Mr Hieu, bicycle tyre repairman, Winter 2004.

Mr Hanh, fortune teller.

Kim Quy giving me a haircut in her old shop in 1994.

Miss Ha under the stairs at Hom Market.

Hanoi Opera House

Ms Hang, my dressmaker at her home.

Mr Suu at his noodle shop.

Mr Dzung, the motorbike taxi driver.

Ms Nga, former housemaid.

Ms Huong, seller at Hom Market.

Vinh's mother, Ms Luu's shop.

Ms Phuong, tea seller.

On her first day at KOTO Hue was nervous. 'The first thing I had to do was peel carrots, but I didn't know how to peel carrots,' says Hue, recalling the experience. 'Jimmy showed me and the other trainees showed me how to prepare pineapples and other fruits. It was a special day.' Jimmy also arranged new accommodation for Hue and she moved to Ngoc Ha village to share a place with three other trainees. 'I had a warm family, something I never thought I would have.'

Hue was in the first group of graduates at KOTO. There were seventeen in her class and six of them still work at KOTO. She loves working there. She has a better life and future and can help her family, but best of all, she says, she has 'a warm feeling and lots of brothers and sisters and a big brother who is always standing behind us'. Jimmy visits all the families of his kids. Hue's parents trust Jimmy and now one of Hue's young brothers has started as a trainee at KOTO. So what of Hue's life now? 'Before, I was very quiet, I was always scared. Now I think I can do anything.' And when you look into those steady eyes, at her sweet little china-doll face with its determined expression, you feel sure that she can indeed do anything.

Dai's Story

Dai is now studying in the fourth class to run at KOTO. He was born in 1982, in Hung Yen Province, the youngest of seven children. His father was only sixty years old when he died. According to Dai it is because he had to work too hard to support the family. His parents grew food on their small plot of land and to supplement their meagre income his father, and later his older brothers, made simple beds and tables to sell. His father used to travel very long distances trying to sell his wares and find extra work.

'I am the luckiest in my family,' says Dai. 'All the others in my family had to finish school at Class 9, but I finished at Class 10.' Dai's school days came to an abrupt end when his father died, as there was no longer enough money. His mother wanted him to stay at home and help her, but Dai had the idea that he could find a job in Hanoi that would earn money for the family. Setting off with some friends, Dai tried to reassure his mother, telling her not to worry and that he would come back regularly with money for her. After two weeks he was able to return with US$7. 'Day after day I worked harder to get more money because my mother had a lot of expenses—my father's funeral, my brothers' weddings, as well as daily living.'

At first, Dai and his three friends worked as shoeshine boys. They all shared a small room for sleeping for which they each paid about US 15 cents a day. Every day they went out on the streets of Hanoi to compete with hundreds of other boys, looking for shoes to shine. There were regular disputes over street territory. Dai and his three friends had to protect and help each other avoid fights at times. 'Others on the street hated me. The police couldn't help me because they don't like children on the streets. So I just had to find another place to work.'

On an average day Dai could earn about US$2. At special times, like Tet, he might earn as much as US$5. But on rainy days for example he might earn nothing. From this small money, after paying for his bed and food, he managed to take money home to his mother. 'It was more difficult for me because I didn't speak English then and so I couldn't talk to foreigners. Vietnamese people pay about US 15 cents for a shoe shine but foreigners would sometimes pay up to a dollar.'

After three months of shining shoes, Dai met some people who offered him a job in their small family business selling noodles and drinks on the street. Dai helped the family and lived with them. 'It was more comfortable, but not more money. I stayed with them for a month. Then I met someone who told me about selling postcards and books. I thought I could earn big money and so I followed him.' His new friend could speak English well, so Dai decided he needed to invest some of his earnings in English lessons if he were to make money. After a hard day on the streets, Dai took himself off to English lessons at night for six months.

Dai already had experience of working on the streets and knew the dangers—the contested territory, thieves, drug addicts and police—but the lure of the possibility of earning up to US$7 a day was irresistible. Dai stuck at it as long as he could, but when he saw an advertisement in a newspaper looking for someone to work in a small factory painting cloth, he decided to give up the uncertainty of the streets and try something more regular. He was paid less than US$30 per month, but he had to leave after four months because of the bad effect the toxic chemicals used in the process were having on his skin and breathing.

Next, he met a boy who was selling lighters and Dai noticed that this person was wearing a watch, looked well fed and was well dressed. His clothes were made of good quality material. Believing that he too could make big money this way, he followed this friend for about a year. Despite his experience, life on the streets continued to be hard and dangerous and he was always worried and never felt secure, especially after he was robbed. Then Dai came upon some information about KOTO. 'When I went to see KOTO I understood it was special,' remembers Dai. 'The people were very polite and it seemed like a family.'

Dai was accepted into KOTO's training program and is now halfway though his course. 'It was a big change for me,' he says. 'Now, I have a second family. On the streets I had no defence but here they defend me. Everyone is friendly, they are all my brothers and sisters. Now I can have a good smile.' Dai shares accommodation with three other KOTO trainees and he enjoys the time he spends with them chatting and joking and talking about girls. 'Before KOTO I had never celebrated my birthday before. It was the first time and it felt very funny. Now I go to friends' birthday parties at KOTO.'

Dai studies hard and even in his spare time he goes to the training centre to read and study English. Occasionally he might watch something on TV at a neighbour's house. He plays football with others from KOTO, 'kitchen versus front-of-house, but kitchen always wins because they are all big people'. He has a bicycle for getting around Hanoi, likes listening to music, 'especially songs that tell about my life'. Dai also likes 'to talk and share life with his friends'. But, most of all he is focused on his plan—to study, get a good job and enough money. 'Even on the streets, I always had a plan,' he explains. 'The others had no plan. They lived day-by-day and would take everything they had left back to their families. But I decided I would keep some money for my training.'

Of the three other boys who came to Hanoi with Dai, one is with him still at KOTO; the other two stayed on the streets, a dangerous option. One of them was locked up by the police during a recent crackdown. 'I was lucky,' admits Dai, 'but I also knew my family was so poor that I needed to have a plan. We had no food, but I saw other families who had meat to eat and a better house and I asked why. I realised I needed to earn big money. I hated being poor so much. I knew if I didn't have a plan I would just stay the same as my family.'

Dai misses his family and his homeland, but there are no job opportunities for him there. There are no factories, no restaurants, nothing except the hard life of a farmer. His mother encourages him to get married. In the countryside even the men get married early at about eighteen years of age. Dai says, 'I listen to everything my mother tells me but I never listen about that. I don't think about love now. I need a good job. After I finish my training I can get a job at a 5-star or 4-star hotel or maybe at KOTO. Jimmy is like my brother now, not my manager or boss. Jimmy has given me a good future.'

Thao's Story

Like Miss Hue, Miss Thao was born in the Buffalo year of 1985 and the two girls became classmates at KOTO. Thao too sold postcards until Jimmy came along and gave her a brighter future. Thao and Hue shared the same miserable poverty and the same happy outcome. But while their happiness now is the same, the detail of their misery was different.

Thao was born in Ninh Binh province, the third child in the family. She has one older brother and an older and a younger sister. Her parents divorced when she was very young and her mother went to live in Hanoi, taking the other two daughters with her, leaving Thao and her brother with their father. This was a sad time for Thao. She missed her mother and life was hard, often with not enough to eat. She didn't begin school until she was seven years old because her father couldn't afford to send her before. Even when attending school she had to help grow rice for the family.

When her father remarried after a few years, Thao's mother brought her to Hanoi to live with her. Her mother struggled to earn a living as a seller in the market and she was able to send Thao to school in Hanoi for another four years. When Thao was fourteen years old she had to leave and try to earn some money for the family to survive. Thao really wanted to stay at school. 'My mother worried about me because I was young to start working, but there was no choice.'

All Thao could do was sell postcards. At first she tried selling near the main post office at Hoan Kiem Lake in the centre of Hanoi where there are many foreigners, but she was frightened of the police there, so she moved to Ly Thuong Kiet Street outside the Women's Museum, hoping to find some tourists. She worked there for almost two years but only earned a little, just enough for food. Sometimes she would go further along the street to where the Australian Embassy used to be located and where some staff now reside. That's where she met Anita, an Australian woman, who introduced her to Jimmy.

'After I filled out the forms I had to wait about three months for the course to start. I was afraid it wouldn't come true.' Thao knew that being a postcard seller was no good as a job, she knew that she needed to change for the future, and here was her chance. In 2001, at the age of sixteen, Thao was enrolled in KOTO's first intake of trainees. She left her family to go and live in Ngoc Ha with the other trainees, but on her one free day each week she would visit her mother and sisters.

At the end of her training Thao landed a job with the prestigious Sofitel Metropole Hotel in Hanoi. For the first six months she worked in the restaurant and then moved to the Met Pub, which she enjoys even more. 'Mainly foreigners go there and people are funny and more easy-going there than in the restaurant,' she says. After two years she still likes working there and doesn't want to change.

Thao earns enough now to help her mother and allow her younger sister to stay on at school, something she couldn't do herself. She has been able to buy a motorbike and likes to be able to buy nice clothes now. And of course her family is proud of her. 'Before KOTO I was always thinking that I am unlucky and that nothing will change. Then I met Jimmy and my life changed. Jimmy is like my big brother. He is so kind and helpful to all the children. I am so proud of him. I couldn't see any future when I was selling postcards, but now I know the way.'

Huy's Story

When he was just twelve years old and weighed only 22 kilograms, Huy ran away from his home in Ha Nam province to find work in Hanoi. That was back in 1993. His two older brothers had already done the same, when they were only thirteen years old. But even before then, life was difficult for the family. In 1985 Huy's parents had borrowed money to build a house, but had trouble repaying the debt. The only means of survival in their small village was growing food as there were no factories, no other businesses and nearly everyone else there was poor and in debt. In 1988, when Huy was only seven years old, his mother moved to Hanoi to sell bread to earn extra money for the family, coming back to visit and bringing any money she had managed to save. But even with just Huy and his sister and father at home, there was still not enough money to live.

When Huy arrived in Hanoi he found his second brother, Cuong. Cuong made him a shoeshine box, taught him how to shine shoes and two days later left him on his own to make his own way in the city. On his first day as a shoeshine boy, Huy had earned nothing until finally, at 5 p.m. he polished one pair of shoes for about US 15 cents. Afterwards he went to a park where he saw a family relaxing together and saw the parents buying lots of things for their children. Huy sat down and cried. The memory of that moment is special to Huy. 'It is my secret thing,' he says, 'I keep it in my mind and when I am old I can tell my children about this time in my life.' But Huy had no time to feel sorry for himself. One month later he was able to earn about US$4 a day, enabling him to take home US$40 every couple of weeks, a large amount of money at that time. He worked at cleaning shoes for three years, capitalising on his youth and small size, but once he turned fifteen or sixteen it became more difficult for him. 'By then I was an adult,' explains Huy, 'and I was considered strong enough to do other work at that age and so people didn't ask me to shine their shoes anymore.'

In addition to all the other difficulties facing a child struggling in a big city, this was a dangerous time. Drugs, mainly heroin, were readily available everywhere. Many young people from Huy's village who came to Hanoi looking for work ended up as injecting drug users and many have died from AIDS already. Huy managed to avoid this unhappy end, realising after a brief flirtation that it was no answer. 'Even when I was little I had hopes of finding a job in Hanoi and I believed that I could reach this dream, so maybe I had more hope than those other boys.'

During the time Huy had been working as a shoeshine boy, his older brother Cuong had moved on to become a postcard seller and, with his friend Long, had secured some territory near West Lake. It was Long who first made contact with Jimmy when he was travelling with a tour group. Jimmy gave him some money and took him out for a good feed. The next time Jimmy came to Hanoi, Long was there to meet him, this time bringing his friend Cuong with him. Jimmy took them both out for meals. Two months later, the boys introduced another friend to Jimmy and by now Jimmy was trying to find a decent place for the three of them to sleep, buying them clothes and feeding them. Four months later, thinking this an unlimited source of bounty, Huy was introduced into the group. 'We thought he was very rich and that we could get much benefit from him.' At the end of 1997, Jimmy decided to give the four boys, plus another he had found, a treat. He took them to Hoi An by train for five days for the Tet holiday. By this time, Jimmy had rented a place for the boys to live, bought them some furniture and pots and pans and paid for their English classes.

A year later, Jimmy added another four boys to the group he was supporting in Hanoi; two of them from Halong Bay and two from Hoi An. 'In 1998 Jimmy asked us what we would like to study for a job, but I didn't have enough experience to know, so I told him I wanted to go back to school. He thought that was a good idea.' This was not so easy to arrange as Huy had finished school at Class 6, when he was twelve. Now at seventeen, he was considered too old to go back to Class 6 or 7 and no-one would take him. Eventually, Jimmy found a secondary school headmaster who agreed to teach him in his house. Huy completed Classes 6, 7 and 8 in only one year, enabling him then to apply for entrance to Class 9 at secondary school. After that, he went to high school and completed Class 12 in 2003, gaining university admission.

After knowing Jimmy for two years, the boys began to appreciate his goodness. They understood that he wasn't rich and in fact gave everything he had to help them. 'We could not imagine that anyone would help us like that. He gave one hundred per cent and never wanted anything from us. Then we understood and trusted him.' In 1999 they had a round-table discussion and the decision was made that they would open a small café, Jimmy and his nine boys. In June of that year, after one month of training, the fast food shop opened. A year later, another joint decision by the group propelled them into the expansion phase. 'We could not imagine that KOTO would be such a success,' says Huy.

Huy is happy with his life these days. 'I feel very strong inside. I believe in myself now. I used to be shy, now I am confident.' Huy has been working as cashier and office assistant at KOTO since 2002 and will study economics and accounting at university, paying his own fees. He visits his parents in their village each month but he no longer has to take money for them. Instead, he helps his sister who lives with him to go to high school. Huy wants to follow in Jimmy's footsteps and help others, but first, he says, he needs to improve his ability. 'I can learn a lot from Jimmy' says Huy. 'He is good at managing and at problem solving. Jimmy is like my big brother. When I am sad he comes and talks to me and shows me the way. He gave me a chance to study and he showed me how to work. He opened a door and gave me a chance.' Huy has learnt all his lessons well but the main lesson for him has been that the first dream is to change your own life, and after that, to help change someone else's life.

These days the tables have turned somewhat. KOTO graduates now worry about Jimmy. 'He works night and day and he has forgotten his own life,' they say. But the way Jimmy tells it is that he is sustained and enriched every day by the smiles on the faces of these kids, now young men and women. 'I have found fulfilment in Vietnam,' says Jimmy simply.

Jimmy had many helping hands along the way, volunteers and sponsors. For more information KOTO has set up its own website at: www.streetvoices.com.au

Christina's Story: Embroidering a Life

Christina first came to Vietnam because her husband was posted there. But when he was transferred to Kazakhstan she stayed on in Hanoi to continue building her small business empire, creating and exporting exotic handcrafted bags to all parts of the world and a who's-who list of clients.

Fashion and law have been the two intertwining threads of Christina's professional life, sometimes one taking the foreground, sometimes the other, but both of them together weaving her life tapestry. From the earliest age Christina was always interested in fashion and pushing the boundaries. She was always looking for something different, something to suit her extroverted character. In primary school she clearly remembers the funky vinyl boots her parents had bought for her and how she couldn't wait to wear them to school. However, the nuns at the Catholic School she attended in Hong Kong were less impressed and told her she couldn't wear them to school. A week later, the weather was cold and the boots were irresistible, with the result that Christina was made to stand in a corner of her classroom all day stamping her feet. When her mother found out about this she asked why Christina hadn't told her. Christina replied, 'Because I wanted to wear my boots to school!'

Another clarifying moment just a few years later was at her aunt's house on New Year's Eve. Christina was asked what she wanted to do and she immediately replied, 'become a lawyer', realising that she had always had that idea. At the end of high school Christina was still ambivalent about her future career and applied to study textile design as well as law. In the end law won out even though she was accepted for both. 'I decided I wanted a professional degree behind me so I thought it would be easier to do law first then change to fashion later. It was a logical choice.'

Christina was born in 1966. Her parents were both Hong Kong Chinese, her mother a teacher and her father a hotel manager. Her mother was a big influence in her life. 'She was a fashionable woman. She gave me fashion magazines and fashion advice and instilled in me a sense of fashion.' Christina's parents were born in Hong Kong in an era where the country was starting to develop as an international financial centre and many foreign companies were setting up business there. They recognised that English was an important language for their children to acquire and one that would provide a gateway to a new world. Christina was a bright girl and was admitted into a selective Catholic school run by American nuns with English as the language of instruction and mainly expatriate teachers.

Although her father was a Buddhist, Christina's mother was a Catholic, probably coming from some Portuguese ancestry a few generations back. 'I consider myself very lucky because I realise now that I had a very different education from my friends who went to normal Hong Kong schools with Chinese teachers. My school was very westernised. Our textbooks were imported. There was a close interaction between students and teachers and we were encouraged to become involved in other things like music, art and public speaking. Other schools focused on grades and the students there had no opportunity to practice speaking English even if they studied it.'

The other big influence in Christina's early life was one of her teachers. 'She was my history teacher and for a time my class teacher. She instilled a sense of integrity in students. She was a strong woman who had dedicated herself to education and she taught me many things in those formative years. She was a very enlightening person and a role model for me. On the last day of study before our big final exams she said to the class, "I'm not going to tell you that you are all going to get good grades, but you will get the grades that you deserve". I still remember that!' And it is clear from talking to Christina that those words did have an influence on her life. She believes that determination and hard work will bring success. 'You have to go with the mentality that you're going to give it your best shot. If I didn't try my best to make it work and it came out wishy-washy I would regret that I did not give it a good try and I hate regrets.'

During her law studies she did internships with the law firm Baker & McKenzie in Hong Kong and Freshfields in London. When it came time to decide where to practice, after completing her professional qualifications, Christina opted for Hong Kong, deciding she should get local practice first, and for six years she worked as a litigator. But this did not signal the end of her interest in fashion by any means. A friend who was editor of an avant-garde lifestyle magazine in Hong Kong asked her to write an article on yuppies. Liking what she had done, he asked her if she wanted to contribute to the magazine on a regular basis. Christina agreed, but only if she could write about fashion, the only thing she was really interested in, and so began her monthly articles on fashion and later another series of articles on career women in Hong Kong.

The only problem with this arrangement was that the magazine didn't have a budget to send her to fashion shows abroad. Instead, they would purchase photographs from fashion photographers who did go to the shows and she would only have these to view. Without being there, and not having any information about the designer's collection. Christina felt like she was writing about 'fashion in a vacuum' without understanding the concept behind the collection. For the next few years Christina used her own money and her annual holidays from the law firm to attend fashion shows around the world with the magazine's photographer so she could write her fashion articles. Clearly, when Christina says that 'you always have to try your best', she really means it!

Of course, these two interests didn't always sit well together. Lawyers are notoriously conservative in their dress, especially litigators who usually dress soberly in black, grey or navy in case they have to attend court. Christina meanwhile had a taste for funky fashion and colours. 'Looking back I realise I wasn't thinking about the big picture, about professional standards and corporate image. I just thought, I'm a good lawyer, why does it matter how I dress?' Clearly it did matter. In her regular six-monthly assessment by the senior partners, the issue of her short skirts and loud jewellery was raised. Forewarned, Christina sat innocently wearing a sober neck-to-ankles dress with no jewellery at all.

When Christina was studying law, a twenty-six-year-old Australian man from Melbourne who was working in Australian saw an ad for a job with Baker & McKenzie in Hong Kong and decided to apply. Christina first met Mark when she was working as an intern. Later, they were to work in separate departments on different floors in the building. At the end of 1992 Mark was sent to Hanoi and Ho Chi Minh City in Vietnam to set up Baker & McKenzie offices. But this wasn't enough to keep them apart and in September 1995 they were married. In December that year Christina gave up her job and moved to Vietnam with Mark. The new scene was set but the canvas itself was blank, waiting for Christina to start embroidering a new life for herself.

In the early 1990s, Vietnam was just opening up to the world and several of the large law firms had come to Hanoi and Ho Chi Minh City to set up offices. But that didn't mean that Christina could find a job easily. Her experience as a litigator in Hong Kong was of no use to her in Vietnam. She didn't know anything about Vietnamese law and didn't speak Vietnamese. She didn't want to work alongside her husband in the same small office and other law firms weren't interested in employing the wife of a competitor. 'After six months of playing housewife I was totally bored and knew that I had to find something to do.'

Initially, Christina spent time talking to some aid organisations who were working with some of the craft villages, helping them to set up small-scale enterprises and visiting the villages to see what they could produce. Then she went back to some of the big stores in Hong Kong to see if she could make a match and find manufacturing opportunities for them in Vietnam. 'They didn't know about Vietnam before I showed them what they could do. They had only used China before. They found it interesting and I spent about eighteen months researching what could be produced in Vietnam.' Christina managed a few orders but the companies in Hong Kong she was dealing with were beset by their own internal problems at the time and constantly changing design teams who kept changing their 'vision'.

In those early days it could take a long time to get a sample right since Vietnamese workers were not used to the demands of export quality. Meanwhile, the new design team would want something different. Frustrated by this, Christina decided she should set up her own company. But what to do? Fashion was her love, but silk clothing was already covered and anyway, she wasn't trained in fashion design and didn't know how to cut patterns. She knew that she needed to export if she wanted a large enough market to be profitable. Christina wanted something that wasn't limited to a particular age group or required multiple sizes, which would mean dealing with different standards in different countries. That's when she decided on bags, and Ipa-Nima and later Tina Sparkles were born.

This enterprise began in 1997 in a small out-of-the-way shop, with Christina and her laptop in the back room and one Vietnamese sales assistant in the front of the shop. She showed her first collection at a Craft Link Fair held at the American Club in Hanoi in late 1996. Craft Link was a non-profit organisation that was helping artisans from the craft villages and ethnic minorities to design and market products with an eye to selling to tourists and export. One of their initiatives was the Fair where goods could be displayed and sold. Christina set up her stall in typical flamboyant style, using hot pink and animal skins as a backdrop to her original and exotic beaded bags. The collection was received well because there wasn't anything like her bags available in Hanoi at that time. Her friends laughed, pointing out that at the fair, amongst all the Hmong, Dao and Thai ethnic minorities in their traditional dress, she was in fact the ethnic minority!

Christina's personality and networking skills got people into her shop, and once there, they bought. They would say to her, 'My God, I didn't expect to see this here!' All her export inquiries initially started through that little retail store. As well as designing her own collections, Christina does private-label orders for big customers where they provide specifications or ideas. From this humble beginning in 1997 the quantum leap came in 2000 when the worldwide fashion trend was for embroidery and beading. 'That was the busiest time of my life because I was able to deliver a quality product that the market wanted. I worked from 9 a.m. until 2 a.m. most days and I remember having only seven Sundays off that whole year. Funnily enough, the staff remembers them as the fun years. They pushed themselves at the time but cherish the experience.' Even today

Christina describes herself as a workaholic. Although she now has thirty-four administrative staff, twelve workers to help with sample development and recently hired a design assistant, she still works ten or eleven hours a day plus four to five hours over the weekend, and sometimes takes clients out to dinner after hours.

Looking back on the early days Christina wonders at how she ever handled it. 'I needed to work hard at it to be successful because I had no experience in fashion or in business. I suddenly made a big switch from a comfortable professional career to having no security. Everything was done by intuition, trial and error.' Travelling to the craft villages was also a very different experience for Christina. In the mid-1990s most of the villages she was visiting were poor and housing was very basic. 'Toilets consisted of a hole in the ground with a brick on either side to place your feet, lots of flies and mosquitoes. I used to try to avoid drinking as much as possible so I didn't need to use the toilet during the trip.'

All Christina's friends in Hong Kong said that there was no way she could survive in Vietnam, seeing only a city girl who liked going out and enjoying the good life. But Christina was prepared to try it for a year, knowing that if worse came to worst she could go back to Hong Kong and get a job. 'When I saw the quality of the hand-embroidery in Vietnam I was impressed and I didn't want Vietnam to lose that tradition. In China these days, it is hard to find high quality hand embroidery that I remember seeing as a child. Most of it is machine done, or else very expensive.'

In ten years there have been visible changes in the villages that Christina visits. Most people enjoy better living conditions thanks to the demand for their work, exchanging straw and bamboo single storey cottages for brick and cement multistorey houses. They have been able to construct communal workshops and warehouses and install fax machines to improve communication with Christina in Hanoi. And the workers have learnt about supplying on time and maintaining quality and consistency, something that took a long time for them to understand after years of supplying to Eastern Bloc countries with an emphasis on quantity rather than quality. Although considered a successful venture by any standard, for Christina it didn't reach the original lofty goal she had envisaged. 'When I first started, my idea was to merge Vietnamese ideas with western design to create an exportable high-quality fashion accessory item. I didn't want Vietnamese work considered low quality. I wanted then to understand the value of their skill so that they could utilise it to make a living and not to be merely satisfied with the low and middle market. But in a way it backfired.

'I was expecting them to learn the process and to create, but instead they just copied whatever others produced. They had no notion that copying other designs was wrong, being used to a social and cultural environment that did not always encourage originality. And while they were quick to pick up some of the business side, they did not always understand the need to pay attention to business ethics and adopt a long-term view. Hong Kong is much easier for doing business than Vietnam.

'The Hong Kong Chinese have a reputation for being shrewd and tough, but they are fair and understand the finesse of business; that both sides have to have a win. Hong Kong has a long tradition of trading and works on a British system and shared values. Vietnam has changed a lot in a very short time. But instead of a naturally evolving system, everyone was trying to push the country ahead and in the process there was no allowance for trial and error. Some business ethics were left out, which I found a bit sad. Other businesses started by foreigners in Vietnam suffered similar sorts of problems. You develop something with local partners and eventually some think they can do it alone.'

Christina tries to protect herself by registering all her designs, but still blatant copying goes on. In one brazen scheme, some ex-staff members decided to set up a completely fake Ipa-Nima shop. When Christina moved out of her original shop where she had operated for five years, unbeknown to her, her ex-staff moved in over the weekend with replicated furniture and fittings. They were ready to continue business as usual on the Monday morning with shelves full of copied bags. They even organised with the *cyclo* drivers from the tourist hotels that if any customers asked for Ipa-Nima they should take them to the fake shop.

Despite a letter she received from the Ministry of Intellectual Property confirming that fakes were being sold illegally, there was no satisfactory outcome as enforcement procedures at the time could not be effectively implemented. The police are supposed to raid the shops identified as selling fakes and are paid by the law firm to do so. However, when Christina's raid went ahead, the shop was almost empty with just a few shells of unlined bags to be found. One can only assume that the shop owners had been tipped off. In the villages where the embroidery work is done, if there is any copying of designs Christina will terminate the contract. However, monitoring of small-scale copying can be difficult, especially as individual workers move about.

Having her own factory could help control production, however Christina isn't ready for that level of investment yet. 'I guess that I have matured a lot and become a lot less trusting. I am definitely more cynical these days. You have to be when you are in business on foreign soil as there are so many issues involved; different people with a different culture and upbringing and a different mentality. You have to be prudent if you want to be mildly successful.'

In 1998 Christina's husband, Mark, was transferred to Kazakhstan by the company he was working for. He had already spent five years in Vietnam and was ready for a change. By that time Christina had set up her business and was keen to develop it further and so they agreed that she would stay on in Hanoi. 'I had already changed my career and moved once to come to Vietnam with him and I wasn't prepared to do it again. I didn't want to have regrets wondering what would have happened if I pursued it. On the other hand, I didn't want him to regret giving up the chance of living in a new place and doing more exciting legal work. It was not easy, but it has worked out for us. I know that it wouldn't work for everyone. It requires a lot of understanding and trust and respect for a distance relationship like this to work.'

While Christina's parents were relaxed about her marrying an Australian, her grandmother needed some persuading initially. She had always feared that no good would come of sending Christina to a westernised school, predicting that she would grow up a 'bad' girl and marry a foreigner. Over the years Mark allayed her fears, carrying out all the duties required by family custom. Later, it was Christina who came under pressure. Her parents saw her throwing away her law career for the fickle world of fashion. Then her husband wanted her to accompany him when he left Vietnam and his parents couldn't understand why she had married their son but didn't live with him. On top of all this, Christina didn't know if she could make a success of this venture. 'My only mission was to make it work. I said to myself, "No matter how hard, I'm going to make it work". I believe that there is nothing you cannot do if you put your mind to it and believe in it and work at it.'

Christina's dream of becoming a big-name brand was given a considerable nudge along when Hillary Clinton paid her a visit during her husband's Presidential visit to Vietnam in 2000. First, a White House aide paid a visit to the shop and Christina and her staff joked about maybe a visit by the Clintons. Then, on the day the Clintons were to arrive in Hanoi, just ninety minutes before Air Force One was due to land in Noi Bai Airport, Christina received a phone call informing her that a VIP was coming for a visit. 'Is that a VIP, or a VVIP?' she asked. 'A VVIP,' she was told. An hour before the arranged visit security forces, armed with metal detectors, were thoroughly searching her small premises, leaving Christina in a state of shock and only fifteen minutes to re-do the showroom.

'We had been told that Chelsea [the Clintons' daughter] would most likely come, but they were not certain whether Hillary would come. I was extremely flattered that Hillary chose to visit Ipa-Nima as soon as she hopped off Air Force One! The shop space was so small and she came with an entourage of about twenty-five people. I was only allowed to have five staff members stay. She had been briefed and knew all about me, about my husband and what we had done in Vietnam. She asked a lot about the business and because she also used to be a lawyer we had a lot in common to talk about. We chatted for about forty-five minutes. She is an impressive woman; strong, articulate, elegant, and I believe she will become President of the USA in 2008. I was so overwhelmed by the whole affair that I forgot to ask to have a photo with her.'

Christina is always designing and coming up with different and new combinations. 'When I see something new, I think, how can I use that in my designs? It might be something in mother-of-pearl, or buffalo horn or ceramic, lacquer or silver. I read a lot about fashion, I think about what I would like for myself and about what my friends would like. Fashion can be fickle and I have to prepare collections twelve months in advance, so it can be difficult to predict trends. You have to find your own vision, believe in what you are doing and stick to it. You can't just do what others are doing or you lose your identity. On the other hand, you can't do totally what you want without an eye on the market. Now we are making more complicated things to keep ahead of the pack. Some of the work requires a lot of labour; for example, on some designs with intricate beading it will require more than fifty hours of work for one bag to be completed as it is totally done by hand. I can have up to five hundred people working on an order sometimes. A large complicated embroidery panel can take one person up to five days just to embroider.' Most of her craft workers are women. The older ones tend to be supervisors, leaving the fine embroidery to younger women with their small deft fingers and sharp eyesight. Christina forbids the use of child labour and pays fair wages.

'The staff who work with me in Hanoi are like my children,' says Christina. 'Some of them started working for me when they were very young and they were very inexperienced. I have seen them grow up, some of them have married and become mothers. I want them to be good employees of course, but I also want them to be able to look back one day and think, Christina was tough but I learnt a lot working with her. It excites me to see them move on to better things, jumping to another level, more than staying on with me with no change. I can't change the big picture here in this country. But I like to feel I am contributing in a small way to the development of this society, that I can instil a sense of standards and values. I feel responsible for my staff. I know that I will always have something to fall back on but I worry about them having a roof over their head.'

Christina never imagined staying in Vietnam for such a long time, but it becomes increasingly difficult to imagine leaving now. 'Practising law was intellectually challenging and had less management headaches. I loved presenting cases and I miss that. Litigation is also to do with pushing boundaries, trying to find a new twist or interpretation in a grey area of law, trying to present a new perspective on things that no-one has thought of before, and that appeals to me. But the creation of Ipa-Nima has been personally satisfying.'

If Christina had stayed in Hong Kong she would have been better off financially. 'I would have a very nice apartment in Hong Kong by now, own any car I wanted, go out to all the chic restaurants and have a very comfortable lifestyle. But it would have become boring. Now, I have opened up to many different aspects of life. And even if nothing comes of it and I end up back at zero, I will never regret this experience.'

A roof over her head, enough money for everyday expenses with the luxury of travel thrown in and a fair dose of excitement is what Christina values these days. As her bags head off to the US, Spain, Italy, Greece, Australia, Singapore or Japan, Christina also travels the world going to trade and fashion shows, catching up with friends and family. 'I don't know where I belong anymore. I am an urban nomad. Living in Australia or UK or Hong Kong is not so attractive at this stage. Developing countries are more challenging but also more interesting and I thrive on everyday excitement. Every day is a challenge. You ask, what will go wrong today? It is not a place for a relaxed lifestyle; just crossing the road is a challenge in itself! But, you also learn to be more patient and tolerant, not to mention to have a sense of humour when things go wrong around you.'

Christina recalls her first visit to Ho Chi Minh City in 1991 as a tourist and seeing the famous Rex and Intercontinental Hotels. There were few cars and the Mekong River looked like something seen in the movies. 'My friend looked around and said, "This place is going to be like Bangkok in ten years' time". I thought, you must be joking! It looked to me like no-man's land. But sure enough!'

Hanoi has changed a lot over the years. After coming from Hong Kong, a concrete city, Christina was impressed with the greenery of Hanoi and the beautiful French colonial architecture. The pace of life was also slower and more relaxing but that could be frustrating, too. These days there are hundreds of restaurants to choose from and not just the handful where you would always bump into all the foreigners in town. The traffic is becoming unbearable. Christina also faces much more competition in the local market.

There has been less change outside the major cities, maybe more billboards. But the rice fields look the same and many of the same timeless methods of growing rice are still widely used, the buffalo to plough, the women watering and suffering the back-breaking work of planting and reaping by hand. However, thanks to people like

Christina many traditional Vietnamese crafts are flourishing and generating reasonable incomes for many of the villages.

The success of Ipa-Nima and Tina Sparkles didn't come quickly or easily, but the journey was always interesting. Along the way Christina met many interesting people. People she would never have come across had she stayed in Hong Kong. She had to change and adapt many of her ways but she never changed her inner values and drive. Old friends in Hong Kong don't always understand why she does it and when Christina sees them in their comfortable cocoons she realises how much she has changed in ten years. 'I don't know how much longer I can stay in Vietnam. But when I leave I will leave a big chunk of my history behind.'

Bret's Story:
A Real Aussie–Vietnam
Joint Venture

It wasn't a long-term dream that brought Bret to Hanoi. In fact, Vietnam hadn't really ever entered his mind at all. Nor had the idea of living abroad. Born in 1967, all Bret ever wanted to do from age seven was be a mechanic. 'My dad breaks out in a sweat at the sight of a screwdriver, he's totally befuddled as to where I came from,' laughs Bret. On the other hand, Bret also believes that his father influenced him and his siblings in other important ways. After a steady job for almost a decade as National Marketing Manager for Tonka Toys, a job that required a lot of travel all over the world, Bret's dad decided to start a new career as a radio announcer in his early thirties. As a result, after spending the first ten years of his life in Melbourne, Bret found himself moving about Australia with his family. As his father moved from one country radio station to another building his new career they went to Adelaide, then Mildura, then a couple of places in Queensland, Tasmania and back to Adelaide. 'None of us has shown signs of settling well, so maybe this love of moving around is in the blood.' All this moving meant Bret changed high schools often. Even though he didn't like school, he did quite well, the reason being that it took time to develop friendships and find 'partners-in-crime'. This lack of friends left him with not much to do other than focus on study, apart from 'mucking around with electrical and mechanical things and riding my bike around out in the bush'. Finally, he decided he had been at school too long. At sixteen he was indentured as an apprentice in a Government motor garage in Adelaide.

After two and a half years, Bret became frustrated with his workplace and felt he wasn't learning enough. Then, on a trip across the Simpson Desert organised by the Duke of Edinburgh Award Scheme, he met a man who offered him a job with his engineering company in Adelaide to finish his apprenticeship. Once he was qualified as a motor mechanic he changed jobs regularly every one or one and a half years. 'I've never been steady with a job. I always like to jump around because it's more interesting.' He tried other types of jobs when he 'wanted a change from thinking about cars and getting dirty'. This included jobs like lawn-mowing, fruit-picking and even woodcutting, though he soon realised that he wasn't really built for it and only lasted a short time.

When Bret was in his mid-teens, the whole family went on an overseas holiday. They went to Hong Kong for the shopping, took a day-trip into mainland China and went to Manila expecting to find beautiful tropical beaches. Instead, they saw the poverty of the country. This brief interlude didn't inspire Bret with any ideas of further travel in Asia, preferring instead to travel around Australia. 'Australia is the most beautiful national park in the world. I did up an old school bus as a campervan and every couple of weekends I would head off in it all over Queensland.'

Bret tended to keep his girlfriends longer than he kept his jobs. At the age of twenty-four he found himself in Toowoomba embarking on his second serious relationship. He says he was anti-marriage and anti-kids at the time, still only interested in exploring Australia and certainly with no thoughts of Asia. That is, until just over four years later, at the end of 1995, when his girlfriend had the opportunity to come to Vietnam with her job. Bret came with her.

'As a kid I wasn't allowed to watch the Vietnam War on TV. But before coming to Vietnam I read a bit of history of the place. I read enough to know it's a place that had its arse kicked over the last two thousand years by various groups and was obviously full of people who want to stand up for themselves; determined to have their own country.' And his first impression of Hanoi? Traffic and driving on the wrong side of the road. 'On the way in from the airport our taxi hit someone. Not bad for our first day in the place! We didn't hit 'em too hard, they got up again!'

After being in Hanoi for two weeks Bret landed a job as property manager at the Canadian Embassy. 'Because no-one else applied,' he claims. 'I had never spent more than two years in a job until I came to Hanoi and spent four and a half years at the Canadian Embassy and set an all-time record.' But while settling down on the work front, Bret's relationship of five years came to an amicable end after six months in Hanoi. Wondering what to do next Bret decided, 'I had a bicycle, a job, I was happy, so I stayed on after the break-up.' Eight years later he is still in Hanoi, still happy, but under very different circumstances—circumstances he couldn't have imagined back then.

Bret had originally expected to stay in Hanoi for a couple of years. After the break-up of the relationship that brought him here, he decided he might as well remain in Hanoi alone as long as he was enjoying life. He had started learning the language, had developed close friendships with three young Vietnamese men he worked with at the Canadian Embassy and was 'having a nice time not thinking about women'. He didn't want to rush into a relationship at that time. Little did he imagine then that eight years down the track he would be living in Hanoi with a Vietnamese wife, two daughters and his own business, returning to Australia only twice during that period.

Bret's wife Hong Anh graduated from the Hanoi Conservatorium, specialising in monochord, a traditional one-stringed Vietnamese instrument requiring considerable skill. However, playing music was unlikely to provide an income at that time and so she took a job as a receptionist in a hotel to earn her own money. She worked hard over long hours, learning English at the same time to better herself. Next, she moved to a consulting and training company where her Australian boss, Matthew, taught her to type. 'The most tolerant man in the world,' she says about him. As her skills and experience improved, Hong Anh found better jobs, becoming an administrative assistant at the Canadian Embassy in 1994, a move that would later bring her and Bret together. It wasn't love at first sight. Bret had already been working at the Embassy for about a year when, on his birthday in January 1997 Hong Anh gave him a small present. 'I'll give you a kiss for that', Bret told her, but as she turned her cheek to him, he said, in rather direct Aussie terms: 'forget that bloody European shit. I'll kiss you on the lips Aussie style.' Somehow this approach worked, as Hong Anh says that she was 'stuck on him after that'.

Some months after this first kiss, Hong Anh was set to go to Paris for two weeks for a training course sponsored by the Embassy. Bret decided that if she was going, then he was going too. 'It sounded like too much fun to miss and I would probably never have the opportunity to go again.' It proved to be the perfect romantic setting for the beginning of this Aussie–Vietnamese partnership. However, once they had the 'honeymoon' as one of Bret's Vietnamese friends put it, Hong Anh's father was anxious for there to be a wedding as soon as possible.

After discussing it with Hong Anh, Bret held out, wanting to take that step in his own time, perhaps showing some of that stubbornness his mother-in-law pointed out to his wife some years later. During the initial courtship period all the protocols to satisfy her father were followed. Bret would visit Hong Anh's home most evenings after work, but her father made sure that he always left the house at 9 p.m. After Paris though, the couple decided that they wanted to set up house by themselves and so they rented a small house in another village, away from the direct view of Hong Anh's family's neighbours to escape being the subject of village gossip. In October 1997, they were officially engaged and a year later, in October 1998, they married.

While Hong Anh's father was keen for the wedding to happen quickly to satisfy social conventions in the village and because she was the eldest daughter and soon approaching thirty, an age considered by Vietnamese as being 'on the shelf', her mother genuinely approved of the marriage, telling her daughter that 'this one is suitable for you'. Hong Anh says that Bret is 'exactly the type of man I need'. She had been hurt before by foreign men who didn't know what they wanted and left her confused. But Bret took his time and was serious about his commitment to Hong Anh and to living in Vietnam.

Bret's parents had met Hong Anh before their relationship became serious on one of their trips to Vietnam and Bret told his mother then that he liked this girl but was taking his time. On subsequent trips to Vietnam, Bret's parents and brother and sister got to know Hong Anh better and they all turned up for the engagement party and the wedding. After the wedding, all of them even went along with the newlyweds on a three-day honeymoon to SaPa, a picturesque town in the northern province of Lao Cai. 'We all stayed in the one room too,' laughs Bret. 'Just as well we had Paris!'

According to Bret, 'the engagement party had an Aussie touch to it, but the wedding was even more Aussie'. Some traditional

Vietnamese customs were observed, although 'somewhat watered down'. The red and gold lacquered boxes carrying traditional wedding gifts were brought, incense was burned at the altar and prayers said to the ancestors. 'My parents did all that too, although I noticed that my Dad was sweating a lot,' says Bret with a smile. This traditional part of the wedding ceremony took place in the morning and about one hundred guests from the village were invited. Bret arrived for the wedding in the car he owned at the time, a Russian Lada Niva, driven by a Vietnamese friend who later became his brother-in-law. He wore black pants, matching black vest, white shirt and a tie. 'Only the fourth time I've ever worn a tie—no, possibly the third time actually!' The bride wore *ao dai*, the elegant Vietnamese traditional long dress, a pink one in the morning and a white one in the afternoon.

Wedding days can end up a blur of social rituals and photographs for the bride and groom. Bret vaguely recalls there was some music, speeches and the villagers came 'to look at us and drink toasts'. But the afternoon, he remembers with pleasure, was given over to a real Aussie 'do' in Grandma's (his wife's mother's mother) garden. It started mid-afternoon with about eighty guests, westerners and Vietnamese, and went on until they ran out of beer and couldn't find any more to buy. To go with the beer, what else but an Aussie barbecue with lots of prawns. The couple's Vietnamese friends all agreed that it was the most fun wedding party they had ever attended, certainly unlike the usual formal Vietnamese celebration.

Bret hasn't confined his 'Australianisation' program to just courtship and marriage rituals. From his earliest days in Hanoi he started to introduce some of the great Australian conventions to his friends. With his three workmates from the Embassy, Bret bought a car and taught them how to have a man's weekend away Aussie style. This didn't include staying at hotels and going to karaoke bars as the Vietnamese were used to. Instead they drove north, camped out in a tent on a beach near the Chinese border, unpacked the esky, the folding chairs and proceeded to fish, play cards and drink beer. 'We were singing at 3 a.m. and mucking around the fire, it was just like a yobbo party in the backyard at home,' Bret reminisces.

At first the Vietnamese couldn't quite take to this strange ritual, but now it has become a much-loved annual event. 'First, I had to teach them how to pack a bloody esky properly.' It is all to do with having the correct amount of ice crushed to the correct size, according to Bret. 'You want to fit as much beer in as possible with the right amount of ice to keep it cold. They would have it half filled with big lumps of ice and so I was breaking my back carrying a box full of ice and not much beer while the rest of the beer was sitting outside getting warm.' He also had to explain that it was important to have a large enough supply of cold ones, as no self-respecting Aussie would drink beer with ice cubes in it to cool it down like the Vietnamese did. Having educated them on the finer points of beer drinking, Bret is convinced that they now prefer the taste when it is properly chilled.

As well as beer protocol, there are several other important, almost sacred, aspects of Australian culture that he has introduced to his group. He had to show them how to make a decent fire. 'Not a fire for cooking which they can do, but a fire for just sitting around and being happy, you know, half a forty-four-gallon drum.' He introduced the idea of going camping in tents, not something Vietnamese would normally choose to do, and also introduced the idea of enjoying a drive out into the countryside on the weekend. He taught them that weekends are sacrosanct and not to be interrupted by work, a good old Aussie practice fast being eroded these days in Australia but hung onto tenaciously by Bret in his business in Hanoi. 'I've probably taught them some swearing, too,' says Bret sheepishly. 'I heard a story about a western guy in Saigon who was found collapsed in his office after trying to work out his accountant's bookkeeping.

Everyone thought he had had a heart attack, but the doctor diagnosed it as "chronic hysteria". That's me, I thought. I just go berserk in my office sometimes! I just pissed myself laughing when I heard the story. It's something every expat trying to work in Vietnam would understand.'

After four and a half years working at the Canadian Embassy, Bret left because he had trained his Vietnamese staff to do the job, because it was increasingly difficult for him to arrange a visa to work there and because he was ready to move to something new. For almost two years after that he worked for another Australian, trying to help him build his business, but when that venture failed Bret was without work. By this time, Bret had bought some land near West Lake next door to Hong Anh's parents and renovated the house on it. He also needed money to provide for his new and expanding family, so when no jobs were in the offing he and a Vietnamese mate decided to start their own mechanical and electrical contracting business.

In less than two years, Bret has eleven staff working for him but he is still struggling to make ends meet. 'I want a business that can generate enough money so that I can divide my time between Australia and Vietnam. And we'd like the kids to go to school in Australia at some stage. There is no easy way to build a business. If I tried to do it in Australia I would have got killed with rules and insurance and taxes. Over here it is the same thing but you are allowed to gradually follow the rules, you are given time to improve and each month we do, like buying insurance or something.'

Bret's staff eat lunch together every working day at a small rice eatery on Phan Chu Trinh Street where the food is good and cheap and, as a staff benefit, the company pays. They have weekends away together, sometimes men's weekends, but sometimes family outings, too. 'It's good to get out and let everything, all the troubles, get washed away.' Bret closed up shop for a week in 2003 and they all went on a company-paid trip covering 2400 kilometres along the Ho Chi Minh Trail.

Hong Anh had to leave her job at the Canadian Embassy once she married, in compliance with Vietnamese Government rules, but found work at the British Council while still managing to look after her home and two daughters. Her only worry now is that Bret works too hard, harder than many Vietnamese she says, and for less money.

Vietnamese are good at soaking up outside influences, especially if it involves a bit of fun. They are also good at influencing others, so the socialisation process hasn't been only one-way for Bret. Bret and Hong Anh's home, like most Vietnamese homes and offices, has a small altar where ancestors are worshipped and incense lit and prayers said. Bret is planning on getting photos of his ancestors to add to those of his wife. 'I think it's a nice simple idea for a religion and it reminds you of where you come from.' He is not so keen on the excursions to pagodas favoured by Vietnamese that usually involve climbing mountains with thousands of others, eventually reaching a crowded, noisy and smoke-filled building. 'I think I got pagoda'd-out early on, although they can be peaceful places to drop into for a while when they aren't crowded.'

In the early days of their courtship, when converstaion between them did not flow as easily, Hong Anh was able to teach Bret about food, to appreciate it the way Vietnamese appreciate it, to really taste it and enjoy it. This is something Bret now values. But the life he chose in Hanoi and the struggle to survive and succeed in business also taught him many other valuable lessons. 'I understand now about not having any money and I can appreciate the Vietnamese more, because I have lived like them. I found that Australians and Vietnamese share a similar sense of humour and Vietnamese will do anything for you.' Bret's philosophy, learnt from his parents, that 'a person is a person', proved to be a good foundation for making a new life in Hanoi.

Bret speaks mainly Vietnamese at home now, although he switches easily into an Aussie 'what's up mate?' when his mobile phone rings.

He enjoys celebrating Christmas with his two small daughters, but he also likes to celebrate Tet, the Vietnamese New Year, with an Australian touch. In addition to the traditional Vietnamese Tet foods he usually has a leg of lamb and some prawns on the barbecue. His house is a typical small, narrow two-storey Hanoi style building, tucked away towards the end of a long winding laneway. It has two bedrooms and small en-suite toilet upstairs, and an open living area, kitchen and bathroom downstairs. He was lucky to be able to buy a piece of land adjoining his house that had previously been used by his mother-in-law for her bakery before she retired two years ago. This gave Bret a small garden courtyard, 'big enough to fit up to forty people for a barbecue'. And it gives his kids a safe area to play, where they can wander from their own house, down the path to their grandparents' house and then out their side door and into their great-grandmother's and grand-uncle's house and garden. And just as their two little girls are a visual mix of both parents, so for Bret and Hong Anh, Australian ways and values have blended in with Vietnamese ways and values until you can hardly see the join—a real joint venture.

Hong Anh has been to Australia twice for short holidays, once in 1998 and again in 2001. On their first visit, the couple spent Christmas in Adelaide with Bret's family and then drove to Melbourne in Bret's converted school bus. Hong Anh says that her initial impression was how beautiful the country was, but by the second day she was wondering where the shops were and the crowds of people. Adelaide seemed rather small compared to Paris and cities in Canada she had visited. And she couldn't eat the food. The smell of lamb caused her to feel sick and she was reduced to eating instant noodles.

But the second visit was a very different experience. She began to enjoy the simple things, the flowers and birds, collecting the chicken eggs. And she could eat everything. Adelaide's small size was also seen as an advantage because people were friendly and knew each other. However, most of their two-week holiday was not spent hitting the city lights and shopping malls, but driving across the vastness of Australia, visiting seven national parks, sleeping in their converted bus despite the freezing cold weather. Nevertheless Hong Anh believes she could easily live in Australia, although she thinks that Bret is probably happier in Vietnam. But where they live isn't so important. The important thing is their relationship. Hong Anh describes Bret as her best friend, lover and husband all in one and appreciates his qualities.

When asked if he thought that maybe his earlier relationship was destined to be just a means of bringing him to Vietnam to meet his wife, Bret just shakes his head and says: 'I don't look at things like that. I might spend years analysing that and get a headache! I just thought I'd met a lady who was suitable for me and her nationality didn't come into it. My wife is perfectly suited to me. I've got a bloody good thing!'

Eric's Story:
The Jewel in the Crown

Eric always knew that he wanted to be an entrepreneur. It wasn't the money that attracted him. His family was well off and he could have had a comfortable life doing almost anything. The thrill for Eric was the vision, the ability to realise a dream and build companies. 'I come from a family of entrepreneurs and I have always been fascinated by the idea that one man, just because he wants to, just because he decides to go in a direction, can provide a living for many other people by following his dream or vision.'

Born in 1966, the second son of a French family living in Lyon, Eric had an important role model in his paternal grandfather. Although Eric had never met him, he was a legend in the family and his achievements were spoken of with awe. Coming from poor circumstances in the countryside near Lyon, Eric's grandfather won a scholarship to a prestigious engineering school, the Ecole Centrale in Lyon, finishing top of the class. He set up a water supply and treatment company, which began the family fortune. Eric's maternal grandfather was also a hero to him. He had been a Deputy in the French National Assembly and a member of the group that signed the Treaty of Rome in 1957 that formed the foundation of what is the European Union today. 'He was a big man in every sense, two metres tall and weighing 150 kilograms. Both my grandfathers knew each other before my parents met because they moved in the same circles.'

Adolescence turned Eric from a cute blond angel into a bit of a demon, the normal teenage rebelliousness against parental and any other control, but maybe accentuated by his strong, hard-headed personality. He grew his hair long, performed poorly at his studies and had to change schools after being expelled. Fortunately, his parents persevered and managed to convince him to stay on and finish high school so that he would have the chance to go to university later if he wanted. 'Thank God they did. I wanted to leave at sixteen and go to work immediately and start my own business. Then I saw others who had quit and who weren't going anywhere. I started to see some purpose to staying at school. My goal was to learn what I needed for my business.'

Once he passed his Baccalaureate at the end of high school and began his four years of study at business school in Paris, specialising in entrepreneurship, Eric had nothing to rebel against. He was living in his own apartment in Paris away from his parents and doing exactly what he wanted, making his own decisions and preparing for his future. Then, after graduating from university and managing to avoid the year of military service, Eric decided to give himself a spare year before starting the serious work of empire-building. He bought a round-the-world air ticket and set off with his cousin, heading first for South America—Brazil, Ecuador, Colombia—then North America, buying a car at the Canadian–US east coast border and selling it when they reached California. Next, they flew to Tahiti and then on to Australia, the Philippines and Thailand.

By this time they had been travelling for eight or nine months. But it was a chance encounter in Thailand that set Eric on the path that would change his life. 'We were relaxing on some island in Thailand and met a Frenchman who was a big boss in Médecins du Monde, a non-profit organisation providing medical assistance to developing countries. He was taking a break after completing a project in Vietnam and recommended that we should go there. This was 1990 when Vietnam was hardly on the map, not even for backpackers. It was just beginning to be talked about; Vietnam and Myanmar were seen as the new frontiers. There were still visa restrictions for Vietnam at that time. You couldn't go as an independent traveller. The only way to visit was to buy a package tour from Bangkok and this guy told us about a small tour agency called Exotissimo that specialised in that kind of service.'

For no other reason than the lure of adventure, Eric and his cousin made their way to a tiny backpacker-style tour agency. They bought a package that would take them to Ho Chi Minh City (sometimes still referred to as Saigon, especially when referring to the centre of the city) in the south of Vietnam.

The pair arrived in Ho Chi Minh City and made a number of friends in the French community there. 'Saigon seemed very romantic, like a "Sleeping Beauty" country with a 1950s nostalgic feel. I enjoyed the way the people dressed, to find them dancing tango, the quiet streets.' Obtaining travel permits and extending their visas, they travelled the length of the country for almost five weeks. They went to the seaside resort of Nha Trang, further north along the coast to Da Nang, to the ancient capital of Hue, to Hanoi, Halong Bay, even as far as Dien Bien Phu in the north-west. 'I remember being in Hue at the citadel and seeing the buildings of the imperial palace. It was untouched and like a jungle in places. You could enter anywhere. There were no guards. To go to Dien Bien Phu from Hanoi took two days each way in a Russian jeep. It was an untouched country.'

At the end of their travels in Vietnam they flew back to Thailand, on to Hong Kong and China. Unable to get a seat on the

Trans-Siberian railway back to Europe, they took the train from Beijing to Hong Kong, flew to London and finally back to France. 'It was a good adventure and a very nice time of my life for almost a year. But then after a couple of months of enjoying my return and sorting photos of the trip I was facing a blank page. I still had Vietnam in the back of my mind but I didn't know what to do. When I arrived I really felt a vibration about setting up a business there, but nothing had clicked yet for me.'

Finally, Eric's brother, who had studied at business school in the United States and was working at Euro Disney in finance and banking, found Eric a clerical job in the department responsible for negotiating with the electricity company. After one month Eric resigned. 'It was a good kick in the arse. My brother did it to make me realise that I absolutely did not want to work for a big company and so I quit and immediately went back to Saigon to start a business. I had kept in touch with friends I had made in Saigon and we talked about doing business together and although it wasn't super clear at first what we would do, we decided to set up a tourism company there.'

Eric's life changed because of a chance encounter with a stranger who sent him off to a tiny tour company in Bangkok called Exotissimo to buy a package tour to Vietnam. Later Eric would open a branch of Exotissimo in Vietnam and eventually take over the Bangkok business completely. Eric's cousin's life also changed as a result of the same encounter. He now works for Médecins du Monde. Eric knew hardly anything about Vietnam before coming here. He had no dream of coming and living in the Orient. His only dream was to set up his own company and he never doubted that he wouldn't achieve it.

Eric had a vision early on that Vietnam could become an important tourist destination, but he thought it was probably a long way off. He started off with the simple idea that if he joined with the Exotissimo company in Bangkok, at that time one of the few entry points for tourists into Vietnam, it would feed customers for tours within Vietnam to him instead of sending them to the Vietnamese State-owned tourism companies. 'It was a basic primitive idea, nothing new. I joined with my friend Denis in Saigon, who remains my business partner today. We were just two young inexperienced French guys who knew nothing about tourism; we didn't think about tourists coming from France or other parts of the world, we just focused on Bangkok as the entry point.'

At that time, all foreign businesses in Vietnam had to have a Vietnamese partner and so Eric set about putting together a feasibility study and finding a joint-venture partner. By January 1992, Eric had found his Vietnamese partner, the University of Economic Sciences of Ho Chi Minh City, which also had nothing to do with tourism, but were willing partners with some money to invest in the enterprise. It took another year of lobbying, until January 1993, to obtain a licence. 'We were lucky with the timing. The Government decided at that time to break the State companies' monopoly in tourism and by chance we were among the few who applied for licences because the tourist business was so small then. We also understood that relationships were the key to doing business successfully in Vietnam and we had spent a year proving ourselves and fostering our relationships with MPI [Ministry of Planning and Investment], the gateway to all foreign investment in Vietnam.'

The Vietnamese Government's strategy in this new era of *doi moi* or economic renovation, was to open the door (not too wide at first), letting in just a few players and not the major international ones, in order to keep control and ensure that the State-owned companies wouldn't be swamped. This way, they could create competition and improve performance without destroying the local industry. They divided the world into five areas and the fledgling Exotissimo company was awarded the licence for all of Europe. The other licences covered Canada, USA, Malaysia and Japan. More than a decade later, the State-owned tourism companies are still the biggest in Vietnam, with only two foreign companies in the top ten: Exotissimo is about number five or six.

'It's hard to know what makes a fashion start, but in 1992 and 1993 it just went "boom" and Vietnam was suddenly on the map! On my first visit to Hue as a tourist I saw the film *Indochine*, starring Catherine Deneuve, being shot there. On the same trip, I also saw a movie about Dien Bien Phu being shot and another in Saigon, both using French directors. All of these films were released just after we received our licence, *Indochine* winning both the Golden Globe award and Academy Award for best foreign language film in 1993, and that was the beginning of the big wave in tourism. Suddenly, fashion in clothing took on an Asian look, the fashionable food in France was this Asian—French fusion, interior design was influenced. And we were the in-bound French tour company for Vietnam. We went from two people with no business to a staff of twenty in the first year and to sixty the following year.' The big years of exponential growth were 1993, 1994 and 1995. And the market had changed.

Eric had initially expected their market to come from Bangkok, visiting Vietnam as an extension or side trip. Suddenly, Vietnam was a stand-alone destination and tourists came directly from France and other parts of the globe. Eric's first idea had just been to replace the State-owned tour companies receiving in-bound tourists from Bangkok. Now, he had a new business in a different market. He contacted a friend in France to set up a Paris office to work with the big tour operators there.

'We were very unorganised to start. When we got our licence the first thing we did was travel all over the country gathering information about prices, available hotels, forming agreements with local opera-tors and trying to learn everything to provide customers with every possible option. Later, we realised that was not the way to do it, when the professional companies came to us with very clear requests of what they wanted. Life became much simpler then.'

In 1995, Eric and his partner Denis decided the company needed to open an office in Hanoi and Eric took on the task. Until then they had been subcontracting to a State-owned company in the north, but he realised they needed to keep better control over the quality of their service. The following year they opened a branch of Exotissimo in Myanmar, then in Cambodia and Laos. Finally, after a long-running dispute, they bought out the Bangkok agency owner and reopened in 2003, replacing its backpacker image with a new image offering the full range of international Exotissimo services. These days Exotissimo is a significant player in the region with a healthy balance sheet, offering a full range of in-bound and out-bound travel services.

By the time Eric moved to live in Hanoi, Ho Chi Minh City had changed a lot and begun to lose part of its charm, a charm that Hanoi had retained. Eric recovered that feeling of adventure he had first experienced in Vietnam. The charm he discovered was not confined to the slower pace of life, the French colonial architecture, the parks and lakes. Very quickly Eric met Ha, who would eventually become his wife. Knowing no-one in Hanoi, Eric set up a temporary office in the villa rented by his lawyer in Hang Trong Street. The first thing he needed to do was find an interpreter and he asked if his lawyer had the CVs of any French speakers. In a meeting that was to significantly change both their lives, Eric found more than an interpreter.

Reminiscing about that first meeting, Eric remembers that Ha was a typical young Hanoi girl of that time, 'wearing an ugly bright pink dress that no-one in the rest of the world had worn for forty years, with white high-heeled shoes and an ugly hairstyle. She looked ridiculous. But she spoke very good French. I don't know why, but I fell in love with her and she changed my life'. As a teenager, Eric had suffered from acne and became very overweight. He also had little success or experience with girls prior to coming to Vietnam. When he met his wife he weighed 127 kilograms and smoked two packets of cigarettes a day. Over the next five years he lost 40 kilograms, gave up smoking, now exercises every day and doesn't drink. 'My wife gave me confidence and because I was suddenly loved, something happened and I wanted to change.' Ha remained Eric's interpreter for two years and then went to France to study for two years. They finally married in December 1998 in France in a legal ceremony, and in April 1999 they had a Vietnamese celebration.

Not long after he had established Exotissimo in Hanoi, Eric's brother contacted him about a French real estate developer he knew who was interested in investing in Vietnam and asked Eric's advice. It was a time when everyone wanted to invest in Vietnam and predictions from all the financial pundits about it becoming a new 'Asian Tiger' were rife.

A group of French investors came to Hanoi to look at a site they were considering for something like a Press Club with offices and a restaurant. Owned by the Vietnamese Journalists Association, the land was in a prime location opposite the well-known Metropole Hotel, at that time still the premiere hotel in the city and close to the Hanoi Opera House. Being outside the scope of Eric's business, his only involvement initially was to offer the opinion that the location was beautiful. But when a Memorandum of Understanding was signed with the Journalists Association, because he was living in Hanoi Eric's name was put forward as the Managing Director of the joint venture so that he could deal with the Vietnamese partner and sign any documents on behalf of the group. It was a complicated project requiring the demolition of an existing building and compensation being paid to surrounding residents.

The relationship with the Journalists Association was difficult. Not long into the negotiations, the other players lost interest and Eric decided to go it alone. He became totally absorbed by the project for three years, just obtaining the agreements and licences and constructing the building even before starting to operate the business. In 2002, under the new investment laws he was able to convert it to a 100 per cent foreign-owned enterprise. Even though Eric ended up as the developer and was the one who came up with the business vision, deciding on the design and the interior atmosphere to be created, and continues to take responsibility for hiring the management team, because he didn't initiate the project and is not deeply involved in all aspects of its daily operation he doesn't consider the Press Club as his 'baby' in the same way that Exotissimo is, although he is still justifiably proud of his achievement.

The rapid success of his tourist business followed by the achievement of the Press Club would be enough for most people to rest on their laurels. But Eric is what he terms a 'serial entrepreneur' and so when he met a Frenchman who invited him to join in setting up a factory to manufacture lacquer products for export, he agreed. 'I like lacquerware, it is traditional, uniquely Vietnamese, beautiful and sophisticated, not well known and very cheap. But we made a mistake thinking that the process could be industrialised. It took us two years to learn about the process; it is technically very complicated to produce high-quality lacquerware products for export. We discovered there are no economies of scale, no mass production possibilities.' The company is still operating with two hundred and fifty people working outside Hanoi, but purely as a handicraft operation. Eric is disappointed that there is no potential to improve, but he consoles himself with the fact that it did provide him with an entry to the homeware and furnishing giant Ikea, which approached him in 2002 about making some lacquer bowls.

'We worked on the project with them for three months but in the end it didn't go ahead. Later they came back to us with a new project to make bamboo flooring. Vietnam is one of the countries Ikea wants to work with and they particularly liked working with us. They don't usually invest in their own factories, preferring to work closely with partners and together find the volume needed to reach the price they want to pay. Now, we have built a US$2.5 million factory outside Hanoi and have a contract to supply Ikea with 1.5 million square metres of bamboo flooring over the next three years. The thing I like is that this is an environmentally friendly product with a look and feel of wood, but it is actually a grass, not a tree, and so grows rapidly. One plant becomes three plants in just one year. If you burn bamboo it releases all its stored carbon back into the atmosphere but used as flooring the carbon stays trapped and doesn't harm the atmosphere.' So even Eric's less successful venture into lacquer had a happy ending with a new and promising company in bamboo flooring.

It seems the entrepreneur bug is contagious, because a couple of years after their marriage, in between having three daughters, Eric's wife set up her own business in the importation and distribution of food and wine. A small part of the business is in retail outlets that sell gourmet foods and wines. One of them, The Warehouse, is near where they first met when she applied for the job as interpreter. Another is opposite the Press Club. The main part of the business is wholesale import for distribution to supermarkets, with exclusive dealership in certain well-known brand names. Eric admires the courage of Vietnamese people in general and his wife in particular. 'She didn't always have enough food growing up and as a result she is very small, but she had the courage to decide to learn French, to become an interpreter, to meet foreigners. She never talks about the difficulties, but keeps an enthusiasm for life and is happy and kind. She has no formal training in business but maybe I gave her the ambition to do something significant, something major. I don't want her to spend her life doing mediocre things that are not going somewhere big. I have seen her evolution from that little pink dress-lady I met in Hanoi to a Parisienne bourgeois super-sophisticated businesswoman.'

Eric and his wife and daughters usually spend summer holidays in France. When he's relaxing there he likes to look around for books and things relating to Vietnam and French Indochina. A casual browse through a Paris flea-market a few years ago started Eric on a quest that was to culminate in what might be considered the jewel in the crown of his empire, the replica paddle-steamer *Emeraude*.

In a shop specialising in old postcards, Eric asked to look through a box marked 'Indochina'. Most of them he already owned, except for three that he had never seen before nor since. Dated 1912, 1914 and 1915, the photos showed two boats in Halong Bay on two of the cards and one boat in Hai Phong port on the third. They were all paddle steamers and bigger than anything Eric had seen sailing on Halong Bay. Eric bought the cards and later, using a magnifying glass, he found the name Emeraude on one of the boats. 'I kept the cards, dreaming that the boats still existed and hoping I might find one rusting away somewhere. And because I like creating companies, I put together a financial prospectus looking for investors to revive the story by building a replica and sailing it on Halong Bay.'

With his tourism experience Eric understood the market very well and had a precise idea of the service to offer. With nothing more than the hazy photo on a postcard, he had a boat designed and found some willing partners. As it turned out, he decided to keep it in the family with just his brother, Exotissimo partners and himself as shareholders, borrowing the capital needed from the Vietnamese Techcombank.

With the business side underway, Eric was still intrigued by the story of these boats and wanted to learn more. He started with the Maritime Museum in Paris, searching for the name *Emeraude* and Hai Phong. This only netted him another picture of the boat in Hai

Phong, a larger version of his postcard. Next he tried searching the Internet and ended up on the web site of a philately club in Australia which had a reference to four boats called *Emerald*, *Pearl*, *Ruby* and *Sapphire* that were used to carry mail across the Channel between England and France at about the same period.

Making contact with these enthusiasts who know all about mail services all over the world, Eric learnt that the boats used to belong to a steam train company that dealt with postal transport. At first he thought the four boats might have been sold to Indochina, but this turned out to be a false trail. The Australian philatelists directed Eric to another association in England that helped him contact the British Maritime Museum in London. When Eric talked to the historian and showed him the picture it was clear they were very different boats. Although it was a paddle-steamer, the boat crossing the Channel was longer and had the paddle-wheel along the side and not at the back like the one in the Hai Phong photo.

Eric then discovered that there was a central archive for materials from all the previous French colonies, including Indochina, in Aix-en-Provence in the south of France that was computerised and had experts working there. This turned out to be a treasure trove of information and Eric employed someone to follow up all the leads. Starting with the name *Emeraude* they found the name of the company that used to own it was SACRIC (Sociéte Anonyme de Chalandage et Témorquage de l'Indo-Chine), a barge and towing company. By searching through the documents of the French Colonial Chamber of Commerce they discovered the name of the owner of the company was Paul Roque.

Next, Eric went to the French telephone directory and got a list of all the Roques. There were 1220. He sent a letter to every one of them. 'I wrote a letter telling them I was the managing director of a tourism company and describing my project to revive the *Emeraude*. I told them how I had found the postcard in a flea-market and enclosed a photocopy of it, and that I knew the company name was SACRIC and the owner's name was Paul Roque. I asked them to call or email me if they were this Roque family. I had my staff in Vietnam prepare all the letters and print out stickers for the envelopes and I carried this 10-kilogram box of mail back to France with me when I went on holidays. I had to order the stamps from my little village post office. They had never seen so much mail!'

A few days after the letters were sent, Eric began to receive some calls. 'The first twenty or so calls were not from the right family but they just wanted to call me because they liked the story and it was connected with their name. They would say something like 'I went to Vietnam two years ago. Isn't that a coincidence?' or 'my uncle went to Hong Kong fifteen years ago' or just that they found the story fascinating. Finally, someone called and said, 'Look no further. We are the family you are looking for. Paul Roque was my grandfather.' And so I went to Paris and met the grandson, and also the son of Paul Roque, Xavier, now more than eighty years old.' The story Eric had been searching for was all there in the Roque family's large Paris apartment. 'They had a large antique model of the *Emeraude*, some china that had been used on the boats with the company logo, silverware engraved with the company name. They even had a one hundred-year-old uniform for the staff who used to work on the boats that they kept in a big box. There were pictures of Paul Roque, a real colonial guy with a big moustache who looked typically French. They gave me a copy of the original booklet that contains information about all the cruises, the places of interest in Halong Bay, departure times and prices, and information about the cabins. I took photos of everything and later Xavier sent me some information about the early family history.'

According to Xavier the story went something like this. There were once three brothers, Victor, Henry and Xavier (the grandfather of the Xavier telling the story), from the small village of Brusque, in France. The brothers went to Bordeaux to find work in the shipping industry. Before the Suez Canal opened in 1869, ships from France had to sail around Africa to reach Asia, a voyage that took at least four to six months.

During the 1850s the French were becoming increasingly interested in Cochin-China.[1] In 1857 an armed intervention was planned and Saigon was occupied in 1859. Inflamed with the spirit of adventure of the times, Victor, who was twenty-nine, and Xavier, almost twenty-three, decided to go to the Philippines so that when Saigon was opened by the French they would be able to get there quickly. Henry stayed behind until 1859 to delay the discovery of their escapade, sending their parents the forward-dated letters they left with him.

Clearly, these men were true adventurers and entrepreneurs. Even before the French took control of South Vietnam and re-opened the port of Saigon, the brothers were involved in supplying the French military forces. At one point Victor was sent to Manila and later Hong Kong to organise the supply of provisions for the French Navy at Tourane (Da Nang). When a ship carrying winter uniforms sank, Victor bought sewing machines and fabrics and set up temporary workshops in Hong Kong, Canton and Macao to fill the order in two months. In 1860, the three brothers reunited in Saigon and set up a permanent business operation there, supplying the French forces.

One of their first ventures was a sugar mill and they installed the first steam engine in Cochin-China to power the mill. They were also involved in supplying timber. When the sugar mill failed, they used the steam engine to fulfil the contract to supply bread and biscuits to the Army and bought a tugboat named *Powerful* from Shanghai to work the river in Saigon.

The southern part of Vietnam had become a full colony of France in 1862. In 1866 the Roque family returned to France until 1870 when Victor set out again for Vietnam and began building his shipping transportation empire. In 1873 and again in 1882, the French military sent expeditions north to open the Red River trade. Victor was interested in transporting the rich coal reserves in the northern provinces near China and began operations as soon as the French had taken control. In 1884, Tonkin (now North Vietnam) was declared a French protectorate.

To document the full story of these adventures would take a book. There were political and commercial intrigues, partnerships and untimely deaths and even an attack and kidnapping by Chinese pirates. Poor Victor, by then sixty-one and deaf, and his brother Henry were held for two months for ransom and forced to sell some of their assets to pay the small fortune demanded. Victor went back to France after that ordeal, leaving Henry to carry on until Xavier's son Paul arrived in 1895.

In 1905, Paul went to Hai Phong. He soon introduced four single-wheeled paddle-steamers for transporting goods and passengers in Halong Bay that he had constructed in Hong Kong. These boats were known as *Emeraude*, with a band of green on the top of the funnel; *Rubis*, with a band of red; *Perle*, with a band of white; and *Saphir*, with a band of blue. Boasting the latest comforts, such as electric lights, fans, bathrooms and even a darkroom for developing photographs, the four steamers travelled four different routes from Hai Phong: to Nui Ngoc, a distance of 120 miles and taking twenty hours; to Phu Lang Thuong, 57 miles taking ten hours; to Dap Cau, also a ten-hour trip; and to Hon Gay, only 32 miles, a five-hour journey. In 1919 SACRIC became a limited company. In 1921 Paul Roque returned to France for good. The SACRIC company disappeared in 1953, before the final defeat of the French in Dien Bien Phu in 1954. Paul Roque died in 1966.

Although the story contained some gaps and unanswered questions, Eric was delighted with what he had learnt. Not only was the story interesting in itself and significant in terms of his plan to revive the *Emeraude*, but Eric could also identify closely with this pioneering French entrepreneurial family. At much the same age as Xavier, but almost one hundred and fifty years later, Eric also found himself, after travels to the Philippines, Hong Kong and China, in Saigon looking for commercial opportunities and adventure in the newly re-opened city. He too, had operated businesses in various fields before coming upon the small postcard that was to spark a romantic notion and start him on his boat-building venture. After a long break, the *Emeraude* would sail Halong Bay once again, operated by a French entrepreneur.

At the end of 2003, just around the time the new *Emeraude* was launched in Halong Bay, a French radio station interviewed Eric about his business and talked about the *Emeraude*. When the interview was aired, a French woman called him while he was in Vietnam, saying that she had heard his interview and wanted to meet him as soon as possible because she had the real story about the Roque family.

'What you don't know,' she told Eric, 'is that Paul Roque had a brother and a sister, and the sister was my mother. My mother took over the running of the company from 1915 until it closed.' Amused to find himself in the middle of what appeared to be a century-old family feud, Eric was keen to hear the next instalment of the saga.

'She told me that Paul and his lot were really "metropolitans", meaning they were from mainland France and not really genuine Indo-Chinese who understood the country. She also told me that my hero up until then, Paul Roque, was mainly interested in women and alcohol and almost ruined the business. It was her mother who kept Paul and his family in comfort after he returned to France. I am looking forward to talking with this woman on my next trip to France to learn more about the story.'

Although his initial interest in the *Emeraude* was as a commercial enterprise, Eric has derived pleasure from the thrill of researching the story. And he still has some loose ends to follow up. He wants to check if the boats were in fact built in Hong Kong and see if he can find the original designs and builder. He still doesn't know what happened to the other three boats, but in the archives in Aix he turned up a police report of the sinking of the *Emeraude* on 17 March

1937, about 7 kilometres from Cam Pha port after it hit some rocks and water entered. There was no loss of life reported in the accident. 'A steam engine is a large piece of metal and so it should still be somewhere on the bottom of Halong Bay, so next I want to send a diver to look for the wreck.'

Eric's *Emeraude* was built locally in Hai Phong in keeping with the original style but was updated to international standards to provide practical luxury. It is 55 metres long with three decks comprising thirty-eight cabins and one suite, two bars and a restaurant. The paddle wheel at the back is just for show and opens up as a swimming deck. Eric has displayed photos and copies of documents and artefacts from the original *Emeraude* on board and has made a copy of the original booklet advertising Paul Roque's shipping empire. This sixty-page booklet includes foldout maps, postal and passenger tariffs, photos and information about the various ports of call, and also a lyrical descriptions of Halong Bay itself. It also has a complete list of the fleet of the House of Roque, which included the *Emeraude*, *Perle*, *Rubis*, *Saphir*, *Onyx*, *Beryl*, *Agate*, *Jade* and *Annam*.

Today, Halong Bay inspires the same awe as it did a generation earlier and it remains one of Eric's favourite places in Vietnam. Considered one of the great natural wonders of the world, Halong Bay is a UNESCO World Heritage Site. Covering an area of 1500 square kilometres are almost two thousand limestone islands, some inhabited, ranging from fifty metres to two hundred metres in height, with a variety of limestone caves and grottos. A geographical and geological description cannot do justice to the spectacle of Halong Bay. Watching these ancient monoliths take shape as they emerge from the early morning mist, or seeing them reflected in the sparkling waters under a bright sun, is a wondrous sight that has inspired many poets, Vietnamese and foreign, over the centuries. One Chinese poet wrote that if you don't visit Halong Bay, you have not yet come to Vietnam.

The idea of building something worthwhile and handing it on, of leaving a legacy to future generations, is an idea that appeals to Eric. His grandfather's story of coming from nothing to build an empire inspired him when he was growing up and he would like to see his own children take over whatever he builds, and develop and expand it. Eric believes that most people living outside Vietnam don't really know much about the country. They still think about the war, or about communism, or else focus on China as the next major player. But Eric sees it differently, being on the inside. What he sees is a country that is politically stable with a booming economy and a population of eighty million people with the ability to change and adapt much better than Europeans.

'Knowing this, I feel I have a secret about Vietnam. I know something about Vietnam that very few people know: that it is a very important country that will become a major player. Vietnam is very ambitious, not just within its borders, but in the region. For example, its airline company wants to be a major airline regionally, with Saigon as a hub like Bangkok or Singapore. Other countries in the region don't have the sort of vision that goes beyond their own boundaries. With this valuable information I want to take the opportunity to position myself in different sectors because someday the world will realise and it will be too late. Vietnam is not on the radar screen yet. I have this appetite for expansion because I have this feeling that Vietnam will become a major player and I want to plant little seeds and grow the country.'

Living in Vietnam is very comfortable for Eric and he believes there is a deep common understanding and mutual respect between the French and Vietnamese. He finds many similarities in the two cultures, unsure if this is a result of the French colonial influence or just that the cultures have a natural similarity. 'Seduction is important in France and I notice that flirting is important in Vietnam. It is not like other Asian countries in this respect. Poetry, art, finding beauty and romanticism are also important, so that not everything is directed to mercenary goals. Food is certainly important in both countries. And when I am sitting in a café, listening to music and talking about women with my Vietnamese friends, I feel we are very much alike.'

Eric admires Vietnamese people, finding them deeply intelligent. One of the important lessons he has learnt from them is to think and behave much more strategically in everything, from buying something in the market to managing staff. 'It goes against my natural personality, but now I try to keep cool and not let my temper take over. Vietnamese use these techniques every day and have mastered them. They see the goal they want and find the path to it, even if it is tricky, without using direct force.'

Vietnam has brought so many changes to Eric. 'Vietnam brought the meaning to my life. There was nothing special to say about what I was before Vietnam. Vietnam brought me all this happiness, all the big changes at the same time, my wife, my children, the success of my business. After not the easiest youth, my life after coming to Vietnam has been beautiful. Vietnam gave me everything I am.'

Nina's Story:
An American in Hanoi

Nina didn't actually visit Vietnam until 1979 when she was thirty-four years old. But apart from the uneventful years of childhood growing up in a small town in Oregon in the United States, there is almost no period of Nina's life that hasn't had some connection with Vietnam,

Nina's father was a pharmacist and her mother a teacher. When Nina was born in 1945 they lived on a naval base in New York State, in the United States, where her father worked in the Navy hospital. A year later they moved to Oregon. By the time Nina was six and a half years old, four more children had arrived. Nina had lots of freedom growing up in a small town of less than 5000 people and believes this gave her the chance to learn leadership skills, although there were fewer academic opportunities than in the big cities.

Despite being small, her hometown held sources of inspiration for young Nina. One of these was a woman about ten years older, who went by ship to Europe after graduating from college. On her return she showed the slides of her adventure. From that moment, Nina, who was thirteen, decided that she wanted to spend time outside the

United States. 'I was going to be out in the world and I started saving money to travel. My parents bought me a piggy bank saying "For Trip to Europe".' This desire for travel was fuelled by other presentations she attended about many exotic places and was given a boost by an English teacher she had at school who remains a close friend. This teacher inspired Nina and several of her classmates to become English teachers. 'She was a role model for us. She also encouraged me to explore the world, having herself gone to Europe the year after teaching me.' Not all of Nina's siblings shared her interest in international travel but her parents encouraged her dreams.

At university Nina was studying to become an English teacher, but found herself 'unable' to learn other languages. 'I had to have a Romance language to fulfil the degree requirements, but I was shy and self-conscious and would freeze up in language class. So I was advised to switch to a social science degree where I could have both a Sociology major and an English major and did not need a second language in order to graduate.' This turned out to be fortuitous. Later, Nina was to use both of these skills and study post-graduate degrees in both areas.

Of more immediate importance in Nina's life was the escalation of the war in Vietnam in 1965 and the political protests going on in America. 'From my twentieth year on, Vietnam was my life.' By the time she left university, Nina had to cope with the realities of a war in which she did not believe. It affected her so much that after graduating and completing her teacher training she suffered an emotional collapse. There were many contributing factors. Early in the war a childhood boyfriend was shot down, although fortunately he was not killed. Her best male friend from high school left university to join the army and got caught up in the Tet offensive.[2] Emotions ran high in her small town. Many people were angry and opinions were divided; one day her mother announced that a friend of her brother's had been killed. This last piece of news occurred less than a year after her current boyfriend had been refused a draft deferral. He had been accepted into the Peace Corps but his draft board said 'no'. He wasn't prepared to go to gaol in protest. Although some people were already going to Canada to avoid the draft he did not take that path. In the end, he chose to go to Naval Officer Training School, hoping for the best.

Meanwhile, after leaving university Nina was 'struggling to keep each day together'. Following Martin Luther King's assassination, she worked for six months on a government-funded training program for poor and disadvantaged women who had no high school diplomas. This turned out to be good therapy, giving her another focus. Through helping others she was able to stop thinking so much about her own sorrows, which were dwarfed by those of the women she counselled.

In August 1968 Nina moved to Hawaii, where her boyfriend was stationed at Pearl Harbor, to take up a teaching position at a junior high school. Soon after she arrived, though, her boyfriend was sent to Vietnam. During this period of separation Nina decided that she did not want to continue their relationship. She sent him a 'Dear John' letter, which he received only after he had arrived back in Hawaii with expectations. However, after a summer teaching intern-ship in Western Samoa, Nina crumbled under pressure and they were quickly married in August 1969, without even informing their parents. Nina knew it wasn't right two hours after the wedding. 'I hadn't lived my life as I had intended to yet. I hadn't been out into the world and I really wanted to be on my own.' After the wedding, Nina and her new husband moved back to mainland USA to San Diego. Less than a year later they were divorced. Nina had tried to be like everyone else and it had not worked. When she went to a counsellor Nina was advised to forget about what she thought she 'should' do and to do what felt right for her.

In response, in September 1970, Nina got a teaching job in Virginia and lived in Washington, DC. She had taken a risk, but was free and on her own. During this year she became more involved in anti-war protests and explored the Women's Movement, finding an intellectual and emotional home in the activism. 'My mother was afraid I was becoming radical and although I was never involved in any legal trouble related to protests, I was sometimes scared.' When Nina decided that she wanted to apply for the Peace Corps her mother was relieved and supported her in that decision.

But then she learned about working on a kibbutz in Israel.[3] She went to live in one on the Lebanese border where she stayed for five months. It was there that she met a Swedish man, several years younger, and they travelled to Sweden together that summer. 'I could have stayed in Sweden but he was just starting university. Peace Corps suggested other assignments but I chose instead to go back to Washington, DC. Watergate had just happened, Nixon was running a dirty campaign and when a friend asked me to work in the McGovern national campaign headquarters, I said yes. Everything in politics at that time was about Vietnam. After the disappointing election I worked as a counsellor at the YWCA for a few months.'

During this time in Washington, Nina continued with political activism, marching against America's involvement in Vietnam and working for women's rights. 'It was an exciting time and I had lots of energy. At that point I had no career or plans for one. I loved teaching but I didn't want to set a career path in American schools just yet!'

With the Vietnam peace agreement finally signed in February 1973, Nina felt it was time to see something of Asia and she accepted an assignment teaching English as a Peace Corps Volunteer at a teacher training college in the southern part of Thailand. 'It was a bit wild in my province as there were threats from local Muslim separatists, bandits and alleged communist groups coming in from Malaysia at the time, but I stayed two and a half years. I taught at Chiang Mai University, in the north, during one summer and they wanted me to stay there but I had to go back to the south.'

In April 1975, the war in Vietnam finally ended. At the close of her term in Thailand, Nina was thirty years old and feeling she had finally broken through the barriers to become truly independent. She wrote in her Thailand journal at that time: 'now I am getting to where I have done everything I need to do. I feel I have done what I set out to do and anything from now on is a big bonus'. Little did she know that she was just at the beginning of her life of exploration.

The world had really opened up for Nina by this time and she wanted to keep working internationally, but not necessarily teaching English as a second language. Meanwhile, she learned she had been accepted into a post-graduate sociology program at the University in Stockholm at the Institute for English-speaking Students. Following her first visit, Nina had developed a curiosity about Sweden, about the way its society had evolved and its guiding social democratic principles. So her plans for studying public health were put on the backburner while she satisfied her curiosity and took up a one-year course of study in Sweden.

Towards the end of the course she got a job teaching English at a SIDA (Swedish International Development Authority) centre, which led to a friendship with Roger, an Englishman who was to play an important role in her life later on. Roger was also teaching English for SIDA. In February 1977, Nina began teaching groups of Vietnamese people from the Swedish-funded Bai Bang paper mill project who were in Sweden for English language and professional training. Later that year she taught an intensive English-language course to the vice-directors and two engineers from the Institute for the Protection of Children's Health in Hanoi and the Uong Bi-Sweden General Hospital north-east of Hanoi. SIDA funded the construction of new buildings and staff training for these institutions.

Eventually, the Swedish authorities told Nina she couldn't stay in Sweden any longer since she had come originally as a student. This didn't worry her as she had already made arrangements to study in

England for a year. Although qualified to teach English in high school, Nina didn't have formal qualifications in teaching English as a second language. In August 1977 she took herself off to Leeds University to study. There were four Vietnamese students in her class in Leeds who were part of a British Council program and Nina became close friends with them. During November, Roger, the Englishman she had met in Sweden, was sent to Vietnam for six weeks to assist the Vietnamese Ministry of Health. His job was to prepare a big group of Vietnamese, who would be working at the two Swedish-funded hospitals, to come to Sweden to study English. When the group arrived in Sweden, Nina joined the team teaching on the month-long program.

Once Nina finished her Post-Graduate Diploma in Teaching English Overseas at Leeds University she was keen to learn more. She decided to enrol in a Masters Program She ended up choosing to go to the School for International Training in Vermont in the United States, since the methodology was the same as that used by the course centres in Sweden. Nina spent from August 1978 to June 1979 doing her Master of Arts in Teaching, still maintaining her relationship with Roger. While she was in Mexico on an internship in the middle of her course she received a telegram from him saying that there was a chance they could go to Vietnam. Another group of Vietnamese needed English language training but the Government was reluctant to send a large group out of Vietnam since it was right after the Chinese invasion of 1979.[4] Roger had told SIDA that he would go to Vietnam to teach there if Nina could go with him. Even though things had been building towards this, Nina thought, surely they wouldn't let an American go? But she said yes, knowing that no other American would have such an opportunity.

In May 1979, the Vietnamese Government agreed. 'I found out much later that the Vice-Director of one of the hospitals, one of my former students, had acted as my sponsor.' Originally, the teaching term in Vietnam was for six months, but in the end Roger stayed two and a half years and Nina remained for four. She was the first American to be allowed to live and work in Vietnam since the end of the Vietnam War.

It seemed as though teaching English was Nina's destiny, despite a few attempts to move in other directions. And it was certainly looking like Vietnam was to be a constant thread through her adult life. 'I was frightened of going there. Why should they accept me? Why should they be kind to me? I had been reassured by Swedes that the Vietnamese Government had worked very hard to separate American people from the American Government in the minds of Vietnamese people. But I wasn't sure that I believed it. In fact, it was true and I had no problems. I never saw overt anger over the war, although I know people were angry. What I did hear and see expressed was a lot of sorrow, pain and hope for the future.'

Nina hadn't expected to be the only American in Hanoi for long. Everyone believed that there would soon be an American Embassy in Hanoi and the Vietnamese Foreign Minister had even gone to New York hoping to sign an agreement with the US Government. However, by October, the United States had decided to normalise relations with China instead.

Then in 1980 Ronald Reagan became President, and the United States maintained an economic and trade embargo, making things harder for the Vietnamese. 'Children were dying of malnutrition and preventable diseases. Everything was in short supply.' About six weeks after Nina arrived in Hanoi, a young American man came to work at UNHCR on the Orderly Departure Program, to be based in Ho Chi Minh City. But he and his wife were never allowed to go there and eventually he left without completing his mission. Later, another American joined UNHCR and was eventually allowed to take up his post. Whenever Nina and he met at functions he would introduce her saying, 'This is Nina. She is the American. I am the other American.'

Nina and Roger taught groups from the two hospitals at the Ministry of Health. The Children's Hospital was not completed yet and the Vietnamese who would eventually staff the hospital and work with the Swedish expert advisers were working in the Paediatrics Institute that was located in Bach Mai Hospital.

'Some of my students had been in Bach Mai Hospital when it was bombed by the United States and their medical colleagues and friends were killed there. Even though the Americans denied bombing it at the time, photos taken showed it was true. Sweden helped rebuild Bach Mai soon after the bombing. In my classes I heard the stories from those who were there.

'In the 1970s and early 1980s Vietnamese were not allowed to socialise with foreigners, we couldn't visit their homes and they couldn't visit ours, without permission. I was extremely careful not to do anything wrong. I felt the Vietnamese government had already been extraordinarily generous in letting me live in Hanoi. Eventually people talked to me about many things as part of our classroom and tutorial learning work.'

There was quite a lot of tension in Vietnam over the Chinese border war when Nina arrived. The Chinese continued to threaten 'to teach the Vietnamese another lesson' in retaliation for the Vietnamese invasion of Cambodia in 1978.

'In Uong Bi, some days there were jet fly-overs. In Hanoi, it was common to see people at lunchtime practising shooting and drills in their workplaces. Trucks full of soldiers were seen on the roads. The Vietnamese Government had removed most of the one-person bomb shelters around the city after the end of the war but new ones were piled up in a park near the Opera House when I first arrived, in case they needed to put them back in. As it happened they didn't, but I kept a backpack ready at all times in case we needed to evacuate suddenly. It was said that the Chinese had promised not to bomb the Uong Bi camp and we kept the Swedish flag flying all the time.

'It was also psychologically sad for the Vietnamese people who had just started to feel their suffering was coming to an end. Many of them had studied in China and had fond memories of that time and friends there. The conflict with China also harmed the economy since the Chinese Government pulled out its development aid and workers, leaving forty-seven unfinished projects. They also blew up the railway's Friendship Bridge across the border, cutting off the source of many consumer goods that the Vietnamese depended on.'

The Swedes shipped in all the supplies that they needed for the expatriates, including prefabricated wooden houses for them to live in. There was a doctor available as well, since there were only three flights a week out of Hanoi and Vietnamese medical facilities lacked supplies. For the first six months Nina and Roger lived in La Thanh Hotel, which is now used to house the offices of international non-governmental organisations operating in Vietnam. Then they lived and worked in Uong Bi in Quang Ninh province for six months. After that, they moved to the Swedish camp in Hanoi, which was luxurious compared to the surrounding Vietnamese housing areas of thatched houses.

At that time there were few commodities and no luxuries available in the shops in Hanoi. There was what was called a diplomatic shop where expatriates could buy Russian vodka, pineapple juice, sugar rations and gifts. Nina had a ration booklet for staples and fabric. The old department store in the centre of the city near Hoan Kiem Lake, a French colonial building with sweeping stairways to a mez-zanine floor, was also almost empty.[5] The Russian and Chinese-built trucks could afford to have only one headlight. Most personal trans-port was by *cyclo*, bicycle or oxcart, with only a small number of motorbikes in the city. The tallest building at the time was the new paediatric hospital and from the top one could see all of Hanoi spread out. 'There was a great levelling effect for all of us who were here in those post-war days. Ambassadors, the United Nations staff, aid project workers and students relied on each other. It was terribly hot in summer and freezing cold in winter. The electricity supply was unreliable so for teaching English we had to bring in hundreds of batteries to run our tape recorders. If we didn't provide students with paper they would write on their hands and arms. And yet this was the life I wanted. I knew it every day. I thought, I could never again do anything in my life that's as intense or rewarding!'

Sweden was highly regarded by Vietnam. The Swedes had supported Vietnam before the end of the war. They were so outspoken in their protests against the bombing of Hanoi that the Americans recalled their Ambassador from Sweden for a time. The Swedes were the major western donors during the time Nina was in Hanoi. 'The Danes had a project for a cement factory, Finland had a project for a frozen fish factory in Hai Phong, the Dutch were supplying powdered milk and the Norwegians had some small aid projects. The French built a new French language unit at the Foreign Language College but there wasn't a lot more. Other western countries like England, Australia, Italy and Germany had embassies in Hanoi, but no viable aid projects at that time.'

In the whole of Hanoi there were only about 250 foreigners excluding the Soviets, Cubans and people from Eastern Bloc countries and Laos.[6]

'For the first four months I was there I wouldn't go anywhere alone. I was afraid Vietnamese people would discover I was an American and treat me badly. Eventually, I understood I was safe and began to enjoy the city. Because most people used bicycles to get around, the city was quiet. Busy, but quiet. On Sundays we would ride all day around West Lake, stopping for lunch at the Thanh Loi Hotel on the way back. The West Lake was surrounded by small villages and open countryside then. In the city, I loved watching the old French trams that were still operating.[7] There were four tramlines but foreigners weren't allowed to ride them or go on the passenger trains. I also enjoyed cycling around the city at night. There was often no electricity so people used kerosene lamps or candles, giving the open-windowed houses a warm and welcoming appearance. At the same time, I realised that it was hard on the Vietnamese to live in the semi-darkness while trying to study their lessons or do household chores. Sometimes, I did my lesson preparations by candlelight, too.

'There was no satellite TV even at the embassies, and we relied on BBC and VOA radio for constant contact with the outside world. The Vietnamese provided entertainment for us. The Opera House was run-down in those days, but wonderful, and they held concerts there. The National Opera and Ballet Company dancers had been to Russia to study and some of them were fantastic. Even throughout the war, the Vietnamese had kept the orchestras and dance companies going. During my time in Hanoi, they also put on concerts of Vietnamese music and dance. To help the foreigners feel at home they sometimes performed songs in Spanish for the Cubans and in Russian for the Soviets and sang Abba songs for the Swedes. Abba was very big in Vietnam! We played badminton at the Indonesian Embassy. I took up tennis after a lapse of many years, establishing a friendship with a seventy-two-year-old tennis teacher who continued to write to me after I left. At the International Club foreigners, but not Vietnamese, could dance on Saturday nights. The Billabong Bar got its start under the tutelage of the Australian Embassy.[8] Mostly, we spent a lot of time sharing meals and talking into the evenings, in our homes.

'We had many opportunities to travel, with permission and "guides" to help us learn about Vietnam. I went to Halong Bay and Hai Phong many times, Do Son, Cam Pha, Den Hung and the Perfume Pagoda, Hoa Lu, Tam Dao hill station, Cuc Phuong forest, Mai Chau, to Da Nang, Hue and by car to Nha Trang and Ho Chi Minh City and around the Mekong Delta. We were monitored more closely in the south. We couldn't take photos at airports, of trains or bridges or other sensitive areas but I have thousands of other slides of that period that I keep in a safety deposit box to protect them. I wish I had taken more architectural shots. Luckily, Hanoi eventually saved many of the beautiful French colonial buildings by giving them to embassies and other groups to restore and maintain.'

Living in Vietnam was an emotionally intense experience for Nina and also for many of the people she came into contact with. 'I feel that in the friendships I made with Vietnamese, we are forever glued together. Whenever we had the chance we talked about life. They told me stories about the war and of their hardships, pain and dreams. When we were together they were often sick, hungry and tired and yet they managed to always be forward-looking. They were also starved for knowledge and curious about the world. I remember writing in my journals over and over that I wished other Americans could know the people here, knowing that it would change others' lives as it had mine. I was also constantly hopeful for normalised political relations, which did not come.'

Nina was glad that she had stayed on after Roger left and experienced her last eighteen months in Hanoi alone, a chance to be 'just herself' in Vietnam. At the same time, when she left in July 1983 she realised that she had probably stayed a little too long and was exhausted. Work had always taken twelve or fourteen hours of every weekday. Living with the realities of the hard conditions of Vietnamese existence, and watching her friends meet those challenges, took a long-term toll. Also, during the two years previous to her departure she had suffered from amoebic dysentery, lost a lot of weight and had an appendectomy in Thailand, as well as ending her long-term relationship with Roger. While it was time to leave, it was nearly impossible, emotionally.

The problem for Nina was where to go after her life in Vietnam. She knew that she couldn't go back to the United States. During her years in Vietnam, whenever she went home to see her family she not only suffered reverse culture shock but also became very angry. By July 1983 she realised that she needed to be among people who had shared some of her Vietnam experiences and that meant returning to Sweden to be with friends she had made in Vietnam. 'I had to be with people I could talk to. I couldn't just walk away from the experience and I knew that in leaving Vietnam I would face one of the greatest emotional challenges of my life.'

In fact, years later Nina was diagnosed as suffering from post-traumatic stress disorder. To help herself cope with the transition from living in Vietnam to living in the West she went to Sweden and found work at the SIDA training centre running cross-cultural training courses for Swedes who were going to Vietnam to work on the health care projects. Although this helped, she felt numb and depressed. Her recovery was helped along when a group of her former Vietnamese students came to Sweden. 'It was fantastic because we could visit each other freely, stay at each other's houses, things we couldn't do in Vietnam. I was able to see they were okay. We developed a new level in our relationships. Before they came I hadn't been able to dream, or at least remember any dreams. I had blocked everything out because of the sorrow of being away from Vietnam. After their visit I started dreaming again. I started to think that it might be possible for me to go back some day.'

Nina stayed in Sweden for three years but she began looking for a career path away from English language teaching. 'Some time after my fortieth birthday my brother said to me, "Why don't you study public health like you were going to?" I knew then that this was the work I wanted do in Vietnam. I was still emotionally slowed down, and it took me a month to fill in the application forms. I was accepted at UCLA and Tulane but I had not lived in the mainland US most of the last fifteen years and did not know if I could re-adjust. I chose to go to the University of Hawaii to study International Health;

something I had intended to do ten years earlier but had put off to stay in Sweden. Hawaii was the right decision. A degree from the other schools might have been worth more academically but I loved the healthy atmosphere of the islands and would be surrounded by people I could talk to. I knew I would have opportunities to study the Vietnamese language and that Vietnamese visited the university from Hanoi.'

It would still not be an easy change. Even after three years away from Vietnam, Nina continued to cope with the losses of leaving. 'Before going to Hawaii I saw a Vietnamese woman working in the airport cafeteria and I burst into tears while trying to order mashed potatoes. Three weeks after arriving in Hawaii I was on a bus and an elderly Vietnamese woman got on wearing the traditional white cotton blouse and black silk trousers, with her hair done up in a bun. She brushed her hair out of her eyes in a characteristically Vietnamese way and I couldn't stop crying for twenty minutes.

'I went to see a friend who was working with Vietnam War veterans in America. He recognised that I was suffering from post-traumatic stress and arranged help for me. Counselling and the support of good friends got me through school but it was a long road to being okay. That finally came after I had studied in Hawaii for a year, when I went to Fiji on an internship. Before that I felt that I couldn't go anywhere ever again. A friend I had met in Hanoi, who worked with UNFPA, arranged the internship, which turned out to be just after a military coup where the government of Fiji had collapsed and martial law was operating. Yet it was a wonderful experience, the people were outgoing, healthy and well fed. Being in another country while learning about health care and knowing that most people were not physically suffering helped me put my mind in a more peaceful order again.'

Picking up all these qualifications and experience, while personally rewarding, was a financial drain. 'My father once introduced me laughingly as his "non-profit" daughter and I couldn't have managed without the financial support from my family at times.' Now that she finally had her Masters degree in Public Health it was time for Nina to settle down to work in Hawaii. Initially, she worked for six months as one of the first women trained to be an HIV/AIDS tester and counsellor. Then in February 1989 she found a job she really loved as program coordinator, then associate director and assistant clinical professor, at a not-for-profit community health centre in Honolulu. She stayed for seven and a half years despite a relatively low salary.

'After Vietnam I thought I would never find anything as "high" again, but working in this clinic was close. Every day was different, sometimes very stressful. There were children around all the time. We covered adult and children's health care, immigrant health care, care for low-income and homeless people and drug users. The centre was established by an Hawaiian Protestant Church when the Vietnamese boat people started arriving. Lots of different cultures used the centre including Vietnamese, and there were Vietnamese staff, too.'

So, even in Hawaii the Vietnam connection remained strong. Many Vietnamese people came to Honolulu on official visits and some knew Nina's former students. There were always interconnections.

In 1990, Nina planned a holiday visit to Hanoi to see Swedish friends who lived there again. She flew to Bangkok to get a visa but unfortunately arrived on the day the headlines of the *Bangkok Post* told that Vietnam had just closed the doors again to tourists. This was in response to political changes in Eastern Bloc countries and the uncertainties that followed for Vietnam. Nina was devastated, but determined. It took her ten days and cost US$600 for a tour arrangement, but she finally got a visa.

By now, seven years had passed since she had left Hanoi, and she saw more commerce and consumer goods available in the capital. There were ice cream shops that weren't there before, and dozens of photocopy shops, and the traffic was a little faster because there were more motorbikes. There were no major architectural changes, but people seemed to be better off and had more food to eat. Nina stayed with her Swedish friends at the Swedish camp and had a reunion at the Children's Hospital, complete with birthday cake. They had remembered, despite the passing of years, that her birthday was on the thirteenth of that month. She gained a special permit to travel to Uong Bi to visit her former students, even though most non-resident foreigners could not leave Hanoi. Despite the current restrictions, everyone was optimistic it wouldn't last and gradually things would ease again, which turned out to be the case.

Nina went back to her job in Hawaii after her three-week holiday, of which only ten days ended up spent in Vietnam. She had used this visit to see if she really wanted to go back. She learned that she did want to, but decided it wasn't the right time for her to return on any long-term basis yet. Once the US embargo was lifted at the end of 1994, Nina felt she could start thinking about a new life in Hanoi.

In late 1995, Nina was asked to review an orthotics project funded by the Vietnam Veterans Association at the Institute for the Protection of Children's Health, a three-week job that brought her back to the hospital and her old friends. Whilst she was there a new friend at Population and Development International (PDI), an NGO operating out of Thailand, asked her to leave her CV. In April 1996, PDI contacted her with the offer of a one-year position as HIV/AIDS Program Manager in Vietnam. The salary and benefits weren't ideal but Nina felt the timing was right and accepted. As it turned out, the money ran out within nine months. Her boss, who also faced the loss of his job, was leaving PDI for a position at the new International Hospital that was opening in Hanoi. He saw an ad for a position as the Technical Adviser of the Australian Red Cross (ARC) in Hanoi and recommended that Nina apply for it. Although she didn't recognise him during the interview, one of the selection committee members recognised Nina. He had been head of the Health Department in Quang Ninh when she worked on the Swedish project at Uong Bi and knew all about her capacity for the job. Nina was hired and moved straight over to her new position at ARC without even a day's break. She held that position for four years until August 2001.

At that point Nina might have moved on to another challenging part of the world, had it not been for a new man who had come into her life. In September 1999, the brother of a good friend of Nina's, an American also living in Hanoi, came to visit his sister. He had been divorced for some time and they now suspect that his sister deliberately planned this bit of matchmaking. 'On the second day he was here we had lunch together and, for me, that was it. It was quite amazing.' They found many things in common. Their mothers had grown up on the Lakota Standing Rock Reservation along the Missouri River, although on opposite sides of it; he was a horse whisperer and Nina's family had always had horses; Nina and John had grown up in the Pacific North-West. But when Nina went to telephone him at his hotel in Bangkok after he left Hanoi, she realised that she didn't know his last name. 'I was astounded at myself. I had agreed that we would continue this relationship without knowing his name!'

John went back to his home in Alaska at the end of his holiday. Nina went to visit him there the following March. They met again in Oregon in June. Finally, Nina told him that if he wasn't in Hanoi by November it was all over, since it was costing a fortune on phone calls at US$3 per minute. The travel and the waiting were growing difficult. Luckily, in early August he sold his house, something he had been planning to do anyway, and moved to Hanoi—not to Montana as he had earlier thought he would.

From the day he arrived John enjoyed his free time exploring Hanoi, soon becoming involved in the Friends of Vietnam Heritage, supporting educational activities related to Vietnamese culture and in the Hanoi International Theatre Society. In his second year in Hanoi, he got a one-year local hire contract at the American Embassy. Then he had another year devoted to exploring Hanoi and other places in Vietnam and now is the Manager of the American Club, a position for which he is well suited. Meanwhile, since she finished work at ARC, Nina has been busy working as a consultant in the public health field, most of the time on long-term contracts with an American NGO working with HIV/AIDS projects.

Recently, after more than twenty years, one of the Swedes who Nina first worked with in Vietnam talked to her about the value of the work she did at that time. He told her that she was 'more than an English teacher, she was a cultural messenger who knew the Swedes' Vietnamese counterparts better than they did'. Nina herself understood that when she first came to Hanoi, 'I was a bridge, intentionally or not'.

During her second residence in Hanoi, while she loved and worked hard at her job with the ARC, Nina didn't feel that she needed to do exceptional things here to feel useful. She felt she had, although inadvertently, already done that the first time she lived here and the dividends from that time just kept rolling in. 'I remember I was thrilled the first time I saw one of my Vietnamese students on the news in Sweden. There she was, making a presentation at a conference in Malaysia, speaking English and on television. All I could think of was the time when she was my student, in 1979, clutching my hand under a table because she was afraid to speak English to the health adviser from SIDA.'

Of course learning hasn't all been one-way. Nina has also learnt many things from the experience. 'I had to learn not to be so stubborn and how to listen in a new way, keep my mouth quiet and not push too much. It was probably good for me to learn to give up control. These days I don't expect things to go smoothly, but when they do it's lovely. I try to make no assumptions and pay attention to signs that help me know what is happening and what to expect. I have learnt to live without certainty and sometimes without recourse and I have had to give up most of the activism I was used to, while in this country. It has been wonderful to have the years I have had with the Vietnamese people I know. Do I understand Vietnam? Not even close to the whole of it. I know more than some do and less than others do. I know how to be here, how to manage and negotiate, and I accept a lot of things that others don't. I know that Vietnamese people have found a way into the deepest parts of my heart. I want to learn more Vietnamese language because I believe you only get to really understand people in their own language. That's why I learnt Swedish.'

For Nina, one of the great advantages of living in Hanoi is that she gets to be with Vietnamese friends, Swedish friends and even some American friends from different parts of her life in the US. 'Hanoi is the one place where everyone comes to me. In Hawaii, the Vietnamese came, but the Swedes didn't. In Sweden, I was a long way from Oregon, Hawaii and Vietnam.'

Nina's life seems inextricably bound to Vietnam. Vietnam was never just a country or a war or a cause for Nina. It was an intense emotional experience that continues strongly today. Her trauma when she left Vietnam after her first four-year residence was the result of her stress at leaving close friends behind, at a time when they faced continuing challenges, and of an overwhelming feeling of helplessness. In the United States she felt unable to do enough with what she had learnt; she couldn't share her experience with many people who would really understand. While she had broken through the barriers between the Americans and Vietnamese in some ways, she had no way to undo what the United States embargo was doing to keep Vietnam from meeting the basic needs of its people.

In October of 1983, three months after Nina left Vietnam, her shipment of books, journals and teaching materials arrived in Sweden. 'Opening that box, the smells of Vietnam were suddenly there in my apartment and I spent the next few hours sobbing uncontrollably, trying to feel the country once again. The next day I put those emotions into facilitating an orientation course for Swedish advisers to the hospitals. Those people remain friends of mine and of Vietnam.'

Nina is a very strong person, but clearly Vietnam has been an emotional, life-moulding experience for her. One suspects that wherever she is for the rest of her life, Vietnam will be with her. A wisp of incense, the way a stranger twists her hair into a bun, a scent, or a face in a crowd will trigger a flood of memories. And the strong unbroken Vietnamese threads will undoubtedly continue to weave a defining pattern on the warp and weft of Nina's life.

Max's Story:
No Boofheads

The saying that you can't always judge a book by its cover is certainly true in the case of Max. If you wandered into his café and tour agency in Bao Khanh Street in Hanoi and saw him in action as a genial host and helpful tour operator, you would never guess at his troubled past. Max was born the illegitimate child of a Catholic priest and his house-keeper (a fact he didn't discover until many years later). Max started life in a Catholic orphanage in Waitara, Sydney. It wasn't until 1958 when he was two years old that a couple were found who were willing to adopt him. 'I had a bad leg and had to wear orthopaedic shoes as a little kid. I was like the fish John West rejects. But my first memory is as a two-year-old, of my adoptive father picking me up at Our Lady of the Rosary orphanage. I remember looking up and seeing the stained glass windows in the background and I felt safe in his arms.'

Max's parents were in their forties when they adopted him and were unable to have their own children. His father's family were Jewish and had been successful racecourse bookmakers until they fell on hard times during the Depression. His mother's family were Irish Catholic racehorse trainers. Ina and Roy had been living in

New Guinea before World War II. When the Japanese invaded, Ina and six other women, with only one gun between them, had to walk to the tip of New Guinea and get a boat across to Cape York in Australia. His father had to stay and fight in the New Guinea Volunteer Rifles. While this affected Roy's health it had a more important impact on his thinking. In his later years he felt he had been let down, robbed and lied to by his government. He had killed people and this weighed heavily on his conscience. He had been told that he had fought in 'the war to end all wars' so that his children wouldn't have to fight. When the Vietnam War began, he opposed it strongly, arguing against the invasion of another country.

After returning to Australia at the end of the World War II, Ina and Roy settled in Randwick, a suburb of Sydney, near where they had both grown up. Max started school in Randwick, but in 1964 the family moved to a war service home in Revesby, a new suburb on the outskirts of Sydney. By this stage, Max was eight years old and enrolled at the De La Salle Catholic School in Revesby. Max describes himself as being at that time 'a cute kid who used to sing in the Church choir and play music'. But that was all to change.

When he was eleven years old Max was molested by one of the brothers at the school. The effect of this was devastating and Max eventually became a violent and antisocial teenager and young man. Unable to tell his parents in detail because he felt ashamed and embarrassed, Max had no-one to go to for help. Sensing something was terribly wrong, Max's father went to the school and confronted the teacher and the sexual attacks stopped. But then, Max was systematically beaten and isolated as he tried to find some recourse.

Eventually Max caused so much disruption at school that he was kicked out and went to a public school at Picnic Point for a while. The family, sensing something terrible had happened but not knowing exactly what, decided to leave Revesby in 1970 and move to The Entrance on the central NSW Coast. Although Max only stayed at school another year, leaving when he was fifteen, there was one teacher who had an impact on him. 'I was lucky to have met him. He helped me in ways he never knew or imagined. He provided me with a reference point much later when I needed one. The good influences always remain as reference points you can look to even in the darkest hours.' But it was still a number of years before Max could pull himself out of this pit of despair. After leaving school he found some work on the Regional Employment Development Scheme, learnt some carpentry and then had many different jobs as he drifted through life, a lost soul.

From an early age Max says he understood 'that society wasn't straight and that everyone is for sale'. His father and two aunties operated as SP bookmakers . They took bets on the dog races, and the horses. 'It was my job to give Uncle Bob an envelope every Sunday. I just thought that everyone had an Uncle Bob, the copper who came around and picked up an envelope every Sunday.' But as well as this education in the school of life, Max was getting a religious education of sorts. His first public singing performance was at St Lukes Catholic Church in Revesby. He studied religion at school, but because his father's side was Jewish, so he also celebrated his bar mitzvah. After he left school his father encouraged him to read to give himself an education and so he studied many different religions in his search for meaning. But mostly he was just confused, believing that if God did exist then He didn't care much about him. 'The faith I could have had was stolen from me as an eleven year-old boy.'

Seeking acceptance in his late teens, Max joined the biggest and most notorious bikie gang in Australia, but that didn't really give him what he wanted either. 'I turned into a really nasty person. It was a wasted life. I had no respect for law and order or for myself. I upset everybody and disappointed my family.' Then Max had a lucky break when he was twenty-eight years old after someone set him on the steps of recovery. Everything changed for him overnight.

But there was one more important lesson still waiting for Max. In 1985, he went to the United States to try to promote and premiere a friend's film he admired. He wasn't successful, but it opened his eyes to the realities of that society. 'In America I saw poverty, hunger and need. I saw a kid lying dead in the snow and people stepping over him. The first thing I did when I came back to Australia was join the Communist Party. My mother complained that I had turned out just like Uncle Ned. But I found acceptance in the Communist Party. I found it stimulating and I liked it. It was full of boofheads and misfits and avant-garde artists and intellectuals. I disagreed with them on many issues, but I disagreed with them less than the Labor or Liberal Party.'

Back at work on building sites, Max was approached to take on part-time duties as a union official and after two years he became a full-time union official with the Builders Workers Union from 1987 until the end of 1991 when he moved to the Musicians Union. During these years Max got the education he missed out on as a teenager and was now able to use his head instead of his hands, which he enjoyed. The Trade Union Training Authority offered adult learning courses that were accredited by the Department of Industrial Relations and Employment and Max attended as many as he could. He studied occupational health and safety, workplace management, industrial relations as well as brushing up on his communist theory. One of the books he came across spoke to Max, so much so that he can still quote the words.

'It was a book written by one of Lenin's foot soldiers and it talks about how to live your life. In this book I remember reading that our dearest possession is life. Since it is given to us but once, we must live so as not be tortured or ashamed of years without purpose, and not be seared with the shame of a cowardly or trivial past. These were great words to me and helped me to rebuild my life and have a second chance.'

The final act that closed the curtain on Max's childhood drama was when he saw a film about the abuse of schoolboys by Catholic priests in Western Australia. Inspired and deeply moved, he knew then he needed to take some action and so brought a case against the Catholic Church in 1994 and won after five years of struggle. This put most of that episode to rest for Max.

Vietnam had always figured to varying degrees in Max's life from the time he was just a youngster accompanying his father to anti-war rallies. One episode that still remains clear in his mind is the day a cousin of his girlfriend of the time came to visit just before heading off to Vietnam as a conscript. A week later this vital young man was killed in action. During his time with the unions, Max met a number of trade union officials from Vietnam who visited Australia and he was active in the Australia-Vietnam Friendship Society, working to have the US embargo on Vietnam lifted. Another of his responsibilities in the Builder Workers Union was to raise money for a workers' health centre in Vietnam.

Then in 1990, Max and his girlfriend Mado decided to come for a holiday to Hanoi. 'I walked into Hanoi and fell in love with the place. I had never felt more at home than here. I had spent a long time not belonging and now it felt like I had found my spiritual home. It's weird, but it was the exact same feeling I had when my father picked me up in the orphanage more than thirty years before.' Despite having had a terrible start to life in some ways, Max believes he has had a most fortunate life. 'Overall I have been blessed and had a charmed life. My parents were the best parents I could have had. I was lucky to have parents at all. And there have been guardian angels when I really needed them.'

Over the next few years a series of events and encounters led Max back to Hanoi. In 1992, when he was thirty-five, Max and Mado got married, and soon after, Mado enrolled in a tourism course. Then one of the Vietnamese union officials they knew, Binh, was awarded an ACTU (Australian Council of Trade Unions) scholarship to study English in Australia and he came and stayed at their house for the year of his studies. He talked to them about the possibility of getting into tourism in Vietnam.

In 1993, Max, Mado and her cousin Helen, a doctor and former Communist Party member who brought much-needed medical supplies she had collected, came to Hanoi. While visiting Bach Mai hospital to deliver these medicines two little boys died of tetanus, a direct result of the embargo. This proved to be a watershed visit. Believing that they might be able to effect some change or at least give support if they were in Vietnam, and since Max had this feeling of great safety and comfort in Hanoi, he and Mado decided to go into the tourism business in Vietnam.

In 1994, Max and Mado started their tour agency, Griswalds Vietnamese Vacations, focusing exclusively on tours to Vietnam, working from a small office in Newtown, Sydney. They quickly moved online, to become the first Australian tour company to run entirely on the Internet. Then Max returned to Hanoi later that year to set up all the connections and subcontracts with hotels, transport and local tour operators in Vietnam. He spent most of 1995 in Vietnam, three months in 1996, and by 1997 it seemed that there was enough business potential to think about opening their own agency in Hanoi and operating their own tours directly instead of subcontracting.

At the end of 1997 they found a place to rent in Nha Tho Street, but after just a few months of operation, found themselves in the middle of a property dispute and had to move. In April 1998 they reopened as a café and the only Western-managed tour agency in Hanoi in Bao Khanh Street. It was a central location for tourists near Hoan Kiem Lake, just around the corner from the cheap CD shops and close to lots of silk and souvenir shops.

Max had no experience in running a business, especially not a café. 'The closest I had come was washing dishes once! But we worked hard, usually seven days a week. The real secret of our success is that we listen to our customers. Having our own infrastructure now, like our boat and bus, gives us more control over the quality of the service we can offer, too. We have more than thirty people working for us these days.' At first they were thinking of calling it the Vegemite Café, but an artist friend did a cute kangaroo drawing for them and so the Kangaroo Café was born.

Max found a high level of acceptance in Vietnamese society and that warm feeling of safety he felt on his first trip to Hanoi has remained. 'I had never worked for myself before and so I am more stressed about work these days, but I have learnt many lessons here. I feel I have become a better person. Hearts get softened here, but you need to stay long enough for the miracle to happen. I have learnt humility and forgiveness. That the Vietnamese tolerate us in their country amazes me on a daily basis. Why aren't they throwing rocks at us after what we've done to them? Vietnamese are confident and capable people and I think it has rubbed off on me, because these days I feel more confident, too. The healing that I needed took place.' Of course Max's political beliefs provide him with another point of connection with Vietnam and he is still committed to communist ideals. He provides proper working conditions for his staff, with free medical and dental care, proper pay and conditions and leave time, and aims for a harmonious family atmosphere in the workplace. He gets angry when tourists treat Vietnamese badly and is not frightened to kick them out of his café. On the sign outside his café where it lists the services provided is the warning 'no boofheads'—a quaint Australian word meaning a harmless sort of a fool.

Max likes the opportunity the café provides to 'educate' travellers with some anti-US propaganda. 'Education is the emancipation of the working class,' he says easily, with a grin. 'I like to tell the truth about things here. What happened here was a war crime. Three million unarmed civilians were killed by the American and allied forces.' The Communist Party hammer and sickle symbol is given pride of place on the wall of the café with the Australian and Vietnamese flags. And Max is even taking steps to become a Vietnamese citizen. He was especially disappointed when the referendum for Australia to become a republic failed and says that he doesn't want to die a subject of a foreign power. He sees taking Vietnamese citizenship as a way of showing his long-term commitment to Vietnam; it gives him the right to vote and thereby participate in its future. Once a citizen, he can apply to join the Communist Party of Vietnam. 'I would love to be a member. It is far from perfect but has made some incredible achievements.'

The strain of operating a small business in two countries eventually took its toll on Max and Mado's marriage. In order to get properly established Max needed to spend a lot of time in Hanoi while Mado ran the essential Australian end of the operation. But the divorce, which was finalised in 2003, didn't mean the break-up of the business partnership they had both worked so hard at. Instead, Max's second wife Hue has been added to the business and the three of them now operate it together. And unlike many Vietnamese women who marry foreigners, Hue isn't interested in living in Australia or obtaining Australian citizenship. 'She loves living in Hanoi. I have heard her describe it to foreigners as "her beloved Hanoi". She enjoys to travel but says it just makes her realise how lucky she is to live in Hanoi.' And that suits Max. He wants his children to be Vietnamese, to speak Vietnamese and to be brought up in Vietnam where he believes they are safe and get a well-balanced life.

Despite the challenges of running the Kangaroo Café, Max has also managed to carve out an acting career for himself, much to his surprise and delight. In 1991 in Australia, Max did a singing spot in a film called *Target Audience* that proved popular in Europe. Then, in 1995 in Hanoi, through a friend of a friend, he was taken to meet Bach Diep, a well-known Vietnamese film director. Then in her seventies, Bach Diep needed a foreign face for a movie she had been commissioned to make to celebrate the twentieth anniversary of the Unification of Vietnam in 1975. Titled *The Flower in the Storm*, the film was a true story about the dying days of the French regime in Vietnam just before their defeat at Dien Bien Phu. Max played the part of the head of the French police. His character was well known as a cruel and vicious man who used to boast that he could break a Vietnamese woman in sixty seconds and had a staff of one hundred and twenty to document the cries and pleas of his torture victims. 'Some of the filming was done in the old Hanoi prison, later known as the "Hanoi Hilton" by the American prisoners of war. Other scenes were shot in this Frenchman's former office and when I sat in his chair I felt my skin crawl, knowing the atrocities he had committed. It was a serious role and quite a significant one and so I felt under a lot of pressure since I had no real experience. But I had great support and help from the director. I spoke English and later they dubbed it into Vietnamese and French.'

Not long after, a French film company came to Hanoi to make a film called *Fleur de Lotus* and found themselves a man short. They happened to see Max in his French inspector role in *The Flower in the Storm* and approached him to do the part in their film. 'I thought it was boring with long bits where nothing happened but it was well received and I began to get more attention.' The film was about the battle of Dien Bien Phu, and focussed on a group of Algerian, Senegalese and Tunisian conscripts who were sent to Vietnam by the French to fight against the Vietnamese. Instead, they defected and fought with the Vietnamese to defeat the French. 'I played a gun-toting French lunatic who gets killed. There was a great shoot-up scene where I had claret poured over me. I had to speak French, but they ended up lip-syncing my part because the director wasn't happy with my French accent.'

Encouraged by his wife and friends, Max got himself an agent in Australia. At first no-one was very interested, until he mentioned his role in the French film. This made a big difference. In Australia he started as an extra, but quickly moved to speaking parts, specialising in what he describes as a 'knockabout rough-head type of character'. To date Max has appeared in around fifty feature movies, telemovies, television series and ads in Australia and Vietnam. 'I like working on Vietnamese films better than any others. I get good roles and the atmosphere on the set is relaxed which brings out the best performance. There are no egos at work, no stars, it is a team effort.'

Five years after playing in *The Flower in the Storm*, which celebrated the twentieth anniversary of the liberation of Saigon, Max played the role of an American in a film commissioned to celebrate the twenty-fifth anniversary. Translated as *The White Cloud Forever*, the story is about a Vietnamese man who dies in a Russian MIG plane during a dogfight with the Americans. His body is never recovered and years later his mother believes she must hold a ceremony at the place his death occurred, that is, at the same latitude, longitude and altitude. The script was written by Bao Ninh, well known for his book titled *The Sorrow of War*. Max played an American ex-soldier who had thought at the time he was doing the right thing for his country, but ended up realising he had been duped, especially after he was shunned in the United States and not supported by Veterans Affairs. He had come back to Vietnam to have another look and apologise. 'It was a terrific script, the ending is remarkable when he brings all the disparate characters together and for one moment in time there is no race, creed or religion and they all come together to assist and empathise with the old woman. It was an emotional movie to make. I thought they portrayed the American character in a very sympathetic light. However, I was criticised by some American expats and one

Australian who thought I shouldn't have done it.' The film got a lot of attention in Vietnam because it was the first time that foreign footage of the war in Vietnam had ever been shown on television. 'It was inserted into the movie as a flashback and showed some American soldiers beating and kicking Vietnamese soldiers and then napalming villages and I did a narration using an American accent that was then subtitled in Vietnamese.'

The Stone Pagoda is a story about the building of the railway line in Vietnam by the French in the 1920s and Max had a cameo role as a French engineer. 'My part was filmed in Son Tay province and Gia Lam near Hanoi. Then I had to go to the studio in Ho Chi Minh City for finishing off.' In a more contemporary feature film, which portrays the difficulties facing foreigners doing business in Vietnam, Max played a businessman. 'I guess you could call it a drama, but there is some romance and comedy in it, too. The films here often don't fit our categories. They don't always have a big climax, but instead look at different problems or themes.'

In 2003, Max was back in Australia for a short visit when his wife rang to tell him he had another film offer. While he was trying to arrange a flight to Hanoi he asked her to get hold of an outline of the script so he knew what it was about. The next day she rang him back crying, telling him that the film was about *his* life. Max then recalled that the director of this film, Khai Hung, had talked to him at length earlier about his desire to become a citizen of Vietnam (and had even written a reference for him). 'He asked me about my family. And so I explained to him that I was an orphan and that my adoptive parents were now both dead. I told him that I felt at home and safe here and that I wanted to participate in the future of the country and that meant voting among other things.

'Apparently when he came to make this film to encourage Vietnamese citizens to vote in the elections he decided to take my story as the basis. They changed it a bit and in the end I became a

British environmentalist working at BaVi National Park. But I was still called Max. I spoke in English and they added subtitles. It took about ten days to film and was shown as a two-part telemovie. It was really emotional for me, playing out my life.'

More recently Max has had a change of pace, getting involved in a popular television comedy skit-type show called *Weekend Meeting* shown on Saturday mornings. 'It's really funny and they send up all sorts of people and organisations and even the government. A while ago everyone in Vietnam wanted to look Korean because there was a popular Korean soap opera showing and so they made fun of that. Even the monks aren't exempt. They had one skit talking about how come all the monks have mobile phones and brand new motorbikes.' Max has done a few of these skits to date. One was called 'The Signature of Mr Phillip' where Max is Mr Phillip, the Director of a foreign company. Two rather dubious Vietnamese characters are trying to sign him up to a deal and try every ploy in the book, flattering and bringing him delicacies, but in the end get bettered by a beautiful young girl who gives them a big wink as she walks off with Mr Phillip.

'The Vietnamese are able to laugh at themselves. In another skit I did I was cast as a German whose daughter had married a Vietnamese man from a very rich family. I was taken to meet the family. It was a dig at the *nouveau riche* Vietnamese who have taken to building ostentatious and ridiculous houses. This family had created a different theme for each level of their house, a Japanese floor, a Vietnamese floor, a French floor, even an Indian floor that you have to climb to by a rope ladder, which I fall from and have to be carried away.'

There are also game shows on Vietnamese television these days with motorbikes as the big giveaway. Max was approached about being the host on the Vietnamese version of *Wheel of Fortune* but declined since he couldn't read or speak Vietnamese well enough. However, he did do an ad for Vietnamese television for a new noodle company. 'When it came time to do the voice-over in the studio, the sound guys made me do it over and over again and laughed so much they were crying, just because I was a foreigner speaking Vietnamese. After it was over they said to me, "We really enjoyed you"!'

Max is a member of Actors Equity in Australia. In Vietnam there is an actors' association and he is working with them to set up a proper union, especially to protect Vietnamese actors from foreign film-makers. Max takes his acting very seriously and professionally and expects to be compensated properly. When *The Quiet American* was being filmed, he was approached but refused when he was told they would only pay $40 a day. 'I told them that the last time I worked for that sort of money was in 1979 on a building site in Melbourne! Not that there was any shortage of expats here hoping to be discovered. They're still waiting!'

Max's first love, which is music, has taken a back seat for some time. His guitar lessons were the one thing that gave him comfort as a child and even in his troubled later years he was singing, playing guitar, and writing his own songs. In 1995 he ran the first Australian contemporary music program for Voice of Vietnam Radio. These days it's hard for him to find enough time between running his tour café, making films here and in Australia, and making sure that he spends enough time with his family. He has some plans to try to make time for music in the future.

After a rocky start to life, Max is now a happy man who enjoys the feeling of living as part of a Vietnamese neighbourhood and who manages to make long-term friends out of his customers. He has found his home in every sense. And his tip for tourists: 'Anyone who doesn't have a good time in Vietnam wouldn't have a good time anywhere.'

Philippe's Story:
A Tiny Hand

Philippe is a charming Frenchman who, before he reached fifty, had already managed to live what would take most of us several lives to fit in. He had been a university student, a squatter in Paris, a zoo keeper, a cabaret singer in Japan, a jewellery seller, lived for many years in Bali, married once and divorced. Then he discovered Hanoi and re-invented himself once more, this time as a family man and successful entrepreneur.

Born in Paris in 1949, Philippe decided to escape the confines of his family by studying journalism at university in Strasbourg. However, there were many distractions for university students in 1968, a period of political and social changes and liberal attitudes to life. He and his friend Ali, who now also lives in Hanoi, were kicked out of university because they didn't study seriously enough.

After that, Philippe was taken on as a trainee journalist at French National Radio where he waited for his lucky break. 'I worked there from 7 a.m. to 9 p.m. and told myself that one day there will be no-one else available and they will have to send me to do the story.' This turned out to be the case and Philippe got his break, but it was a short-lived victory. There were rules about what could and could not be said on air that had to be followed, something Philippe couldn't always guarantee, and so after six months his contract was not renewed.

During the decade from 1968 to 1978, Philippe lived a bohemian existence, moving as the mood took him, living from hand to mouth, turning his hand to whatever turned up with no long-term plan. 'My friends and I didn't want a career, a normal life with a wife and kids and the same job for forty-five years. And the future proved us not so wrong. After that time, unemployment became a problem and no-one believes they are guaranteed work for a lifetime anymore.' Philippe's parents warned him about placing too much importance on friendship, but he didn't accept their view. 'Friends became my real family and we all shared the dreams of the time for a different life and a different world.'

Whilst he was a student, Philippe began singing in bars and cafes and discovered to his surprise that he could earn one-quarter of his monthly living expenses in one night. He went back to singing with a friend after leaving the radio job and continued on and off for a number of years. For a year in 1972 and 1973 he went to the south of France and lived there in a commune with about ten people. When he got tired of that, he decided to go to St Tropez in the hope of finding some work for the summer. He had no money at all and had expected to hitch a ride there, but with his long hair and beard no-one wanted to pick him up. It took him two days and nights to walk and he survived by stealing fruit and vegetables from gardens. When he arrived, the only job he could find was selling ice cream on the beach. 'It is not easy carrying twenty-five kilograms of ice cream while walking on sand. I used to sleep on the beach and in two or three months managed to save some money.'

In 1973, Philippe visited Indonesia for his brother's wedding. His brother was living and working in Indonesia at the time and married a French woman. 'I had a strong reaction to Indonesia—I loved it. I stayed for three months but ran out of money so I came back to Paris, planning to return in six months. But I never managed to raise enough money to return at that time.' From then on Philippe had a string of short-lived jobs. At one time he was selling fruit and vegetables and living in a squat in Paris as a political statement against the wastefulness of empty public buildings. 'Do you know the most painful vegetable to handle? Mushrooms in the cold weather because they are soft and get under your fingernails and freeze. It is torture and your fingers bleed.'

Another time he worked in the zoo inside the Jardin des Plantes, a well-known garden in the centre of Paris. 'I needed money to live, but quality of life has always been my first concern, so when I was walking through the Jardin des Plantes one day I thought it would be nice to work there amongst the trees and plants. I saw the administration building and went in. The girl there asked me if I had come for the job. Of course I said yes, even thought I didn't know what the job was. Then she asked if I was a university graduate. When I told her only two years, she said that was too much since the job only required someone to feed the animals in the zoo. The main skill they wanted was someone who could drive a tractor. "Do you drive a tractor?" she asked. "I was almost born on a tractor with my grandfather", I replied, having never even known my grandfather let alone driven a tractor. I wanted that job. I am probably the only person who learnt how to drive a tractor in Paris! For the most part it was a pleasant job, I liked driving the tractor and having all the animals greet me when I brought their feed. The worst part was cleaning the lion's den, nothing smells as bad as lion shit!'

One day in 1977 Philippe saw an ad in the newspaper looking for a French singer for a cabaret in Tokyo. At that time he was living with his older brother who had now returned from Indonesia. 'I was the black sheep of the family, living a marginal life. My brother and my sister were mainstream. When my brother saw the ad he told me that if I didn't try for the job he would kick me out. He complained that I was a dreamer and that I wasn't trying for anything because that meant that I couldn't fail. Now I had to prove to him that I had tried something. When I arrived and saw the queue waiting to audition I wanted to leave, but I had to take proof to my brother that I had tried. I was number 256, which meant there were 255 ahead of me and probably the same number behind; so I didn't like my chances. I waited four or five hours and sang for a Japanese guy and a French guy. They asked for a second song and took a photo. I asked them for a stamp so I could show my brother to prove I had auditioned. My brother was happy that I had tried and we held a small party that night. The result wasn't until the next day but if we waited we feared there would be nothing to celebrate. This way there was still hope. We drank all night until 5 a.m. At 8 a.m. the telephone rang. I had been chosen and they wanted me to come and sign the contract in one hour. 'Could I come this afternoon?' I asked. The reply was that if I wanted to work for a Japanese company then I should be there in one hour. And so I was, and ten days later I left for Japan.'

Philippe worked in the Tokyo cabaret for six months and enjoyed the experience. 'The Japanese girls like French men and there were a few thousand posters of my face all over Tokyo, in the subways and taxis. The experience changed my life in some ways. I became more confident and I learnt to be honest. Before I wasn't always so honest and took what I thought I deserved. I also learnt politeness, which is the basis of Japanese society.' He also met another Frenchman there, also called Philippe, who was to become a close friend and later a business partner.

On one of his stays in the south of France, Philippe bought very cheaply a derelict one-room building on a small block in a region of almost desert except for aromatic herbs and lavender that grow wild. He invested his small savings in this property so that he would always have somewhere to go when he returned from Japan. He spent some of the money he earned from his cabaret singing on repairing the building to make it liveable. He also went to visit his sister who was living in Montreal, did some singing there for a few months, but ran away when the cold of winter arrived.

Life changed for Philippe in 1978. In that year he opened a jewellery stall in the subway, his first experience in business. For someone who enjoys the outdoors and loves trees and plants this was a hard job, being underground twelve hours a day, seven days a week. But importantly, it was successful and set him on the path to owning a number of jewellery shops over the next twenty years. It was also in the subway that he met his first wife by chance. 'I had 500,000 people passing my stall every day so I had to be able to find somebody!' he jokes. They married in 1978 when he was twenty-nine and she was only eighteen. He also met up again with his friend Philippe from Tokyo and they decided to go into business together wholesaling necklaces produced in the Philippines. In the summer of 1978 they went to the Philippines together for three months and bought 8000 necklaces of the same design. The next year they bought the entire production of six months, around 350,000 pieces, on credit, and they had to employ people to sell them on the beaches in France during the summer, as well as selling to wholesalers and retailers.

The profits from this venture allowed Philippe to open the first of his proper shops selling jewellery and gifts in the old quarter of Paris, where he introduced a different style of displaying stock. 'When I had only a one metre long table to display stock in the subway I had to learn to show as many designs as possible. When I moved to a shop I filled my window in the same way. Before that time, Paris jewellery shops would have only fifteen or twenty items nicely displayed in their window.'

The Philippines connection continued for another couple of years, once inventing successfully a fake turquoise necklace, but failing the next year to create viable fake ivory in a bid to deter the cruel killing of elephants. After that, Philippe stopped going to the Philippines and turned his attention back to Bali. Over the next fifteen years, he began spending more and more of his time there, leaving the management of his jewellery shop to others. 'I only really needed to stay in Bali for two months each year for buying stock but I loved the place and spent six or seven months a year there. It's probably why I didn't make a lot of money, but I was very happy. I learned to speak Indonesian and became very interested in the culture, especially some of the primitive religions and rituals practised.' While Philippe's business continued, his marriage didn't. After about seven years he and his wife went their separate ways.

Although he wasn't doing so much singing, Philippe was always writing poetry and songs for himself and sometimes reciting his poems in poetry bars that had become popular. He met some musicians who liked the way he delivered his poetry and thus began a connection and collaboration that resulted in the production of a CD. But Philippe's destiny was not to be in the world of entertainment. Fate had something else altogether in mind in a country he had only read about.

In 1996, Philippe was invited to go on a motorbike trip around North Vietnam with a small group of his friends. That was when he first saw Hanoi and fell in love with the place. 'Vietnam has a particular charm for the French, especially of my generation. As a teenager I read many French novels about Indochina, describing the cities and the lives of people, so when I saw those things that I had read about and saw they were exactly as described, the conical hats for instance, then I felt a return of those early sensations. I was only five years old when the French were fighting at Dien Bien Phu, but even when I was ten years old I remember people talking about how romantic it

Mrs Nga, celebrating receiving her Henley MBA in London with her classmate.

A motorbike repair class at Mr Thac's Vocational Training School.

A tailoring class at Mr Thac's Vocational Training School.

Christina.

Interior of Christina's showroom at Ipa-Nima.

The new Emeraude on Halong Bay.

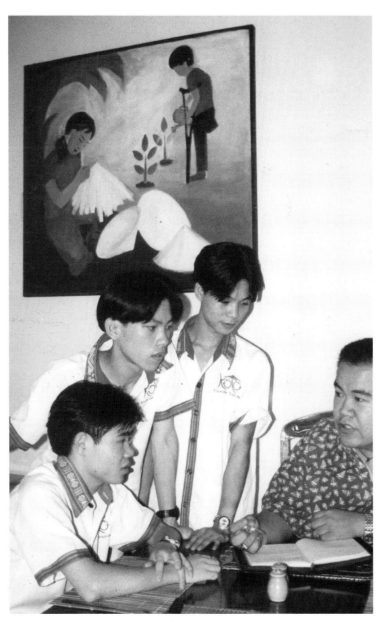

Jimmy with some KOTO students.

Jimmy with Miss Hue and another KOTO graduate.

Carla and Leonardo's restaurant Mediterraneo.

John and his friend Thanh plotting new adventures.

Stephanie and her daughter Tiana.

Hoan Kiem lake in the centre of Hanoi.

Don fiddling in Hanoi with another of the Social Weevils

seemed. Hanoi is full of beautiful French colonial architecture, lots of trees and beautiful girls wearing the traditional dress (*ao dai*). Other Asian capitals I knew were all horrible. But Bangkok is getting better, Manila and Jakarta are awful and Singapore is too clean. But when I saw Hanoi, I thought, it's a dream.'

Philippe and his four friends spent three weeks riding around the countryside, having an adventure with no guide and no knowledge of Vietnamese language. 'We got lost as we knew we would and shared some beautiful moments.' The trip had been such a success that it was decided to repeat it as a regular annual event. Philippe couldn't make it the next year, but turned up again in 1998 and 1999. Three small doses were all it took for the magic to do its work and captivate him.

It was at the end of his 1999 visit that Philippe met the woman whom he would soon marry. 'Hang was working in a small shop in Hang Gai Street selling local crafts to tourists. I was her most difficult customer. I would come every day and try to bargain the price down lower. I was terrible.'

Philippe told her that he had seen lots of things that he wanted to take back to sell in France when he was travelling around the northern mountainous regions, where many of the ethnic minorities lived. He told her he planned to return to SaPa in a few months on a buying trip. Philippe did return to Hanoi in March 2000 and went directly to see Hang to ask if she would go to SaPa with him and help communicate with the sellers there. She agreed, bringing along her two sisters as chaperones. 'Fifteen minutes out of Hanoi all three of them were car sick and at the end of the twelve-hour winding drive when we arrived in SaPa, they couldn't walk or stand up, they were so ill.'

The next morning, Philippe went for a walk in the small town and was quickly surrounded by the local Hmong and Dao tribespeople trying to sell him their weavings and embroideries. 'They were pushing things in my face and I felt like I couldn't breathe. And then I saw a little hand come through the crowd. It was Hang. "Come here" she said, and she took my hand and dragged me away from the mob. In that moment I felt happiness. It was as if this little hand was saving me—not that I was in any danger! I don't know why, but I felt a great emotion.' They spent two days in SaPa, enjoying the scenery and making purchases. Once they arrived back in Hanoi, Hang refused the payment Philippe had agreed to pay her. 'She said to me, "Now we are friends and I don't take money from friends". I thought, this is not what people told me about Vietnam!'

Later, Philippe went to see his Italian friend Gino, who ran a restaurant in Hanoi, and told him the story. Gino warned him, 'Philippe, be careful, this one, you know, she want to marry you!' But by then the warning was too late because Philippe was already in love. 'I decided one day to go on a motorbike trip on my own to explore around Mai Chau. On the way back to Hanoi I saw some peach trees in blossom and remembered that in SaPa Hang had said how much she liked peach blossoms. So I cut off a branch and tied it to my motorbike to take back to Hanoi for her. It was raining and the roads were muddy. By the time I reached her shop in Hanoi and presented it to her there was only one blossom left on this mud-covered stick. She looked and laughed, and later told me that's when she fell in love. It was too stupid and crazy.'

Philippe went back to France at the end of this short trip but he soon realised he was missing Vietnam and Hang. Three weeks later he decided to return to Hanoi, not realising straight away the path he was treading and that he was actually going to end up living in Hanoi. After Philippe had been living in Hanoi for three months, Hang issued an ultimatum. Their relationship had to stop or else they would have to get married since her reputation was at risk being seen with a foreigner in this still conservative, traditional society. In June 2000, after a whirlwind romance, they were married. It was Gino, the friend who had first foreseen where this relationship was heading, who lent Philippe the money for the wedding reception. 'I still had my shop in Paris but it only covered costs and I had already spent a lot with all these trips between Hanoi and Paris. Fortunately, the wedding envelopes [containing money] that the guests gave covered the amount spent on the wedding reception so that I could repay Gino and he in turn could pay his suppliers at the end of that month.'

Before his marriage, Philippe had begun to look for a shop to rent in Hanoi to start a business in partnership with Hang. 'I didn't do anything very original here, it was just the same as running a shop in France. But I was experienced. I had learnt from my mistakes and had a good idea about what sells. My wife is very good at administration, managing, checking, accounting and stock management, all the things I don't like doing at all. I am good at buying and decorating and arranging stock. So we were a good team. I opened the first shop in Nha Tho Street. It cost me US$3000 all up for stock, fittings and decoration. In the first month of trading our turnover was US $4000 and so very quickly the shop was running well. Then I started wholesaling to France. I went to Laos and bought Lao silk. By the second year we were making very good money.'

The first shop that Philippe opened was in a Government-owned building that was supposed to be demolished years ago. 'Every few months there is a new scenario, but nothing happens. One day I expect it will be destroyed. I opened my other shops because I was afraid it would happen suddenly without warning. After months of looking, my wife found a shop in Nha Chung Street just around the corner from the first shop and down the road from the Catholic Cathedral. She came to tell me she had rented it and that now we had to decorate it. I told her I would need to think about it. She told me, "Think about it on the way as we walk around the corner because the workers are there, ready to start!" With Vietnamese you can wait months and months for something to happen and then suddenly, when it is time, you have to be ready to move! I didn't know what I would do, I hadn't seen the building, the shop space, and it was only a short 200-metre walk for thinking time. As I passed by the cathedral I looked at the beautiful doors and so I decided to use that shape around the walls.' A divine inspiration! The final effect was so stunning that the local décor magazine *Nha Dep* featured the shop interior on its cover.

After opening a third shop, this time in Hang Trong Street, 200 metres the other way from the first shop, Philippe decided that was enough. Until suddenly, an opportunity presented itself to rent a large shop in Hang Gai Street, opposite the tiny shop where Philippe first met Hang when she used to work there nine hours a day, seven days a week for about US$30 a month. 'She couldn't say no to the chance to come back to the same street in a big shop, as the big boss, earning big money.'

Philippe has also given a small hand to the other members of Hang's family, helping them open their own shops. 'At the beginning no-one had much money, we all helped each other.' Hang's parents are divorced and her father, who used to be a truck driver before he retired, lives alone in a tiny fourteen-square metre, two-roomed building. 'I give him money but he gives it away. He says he needs nothing. He owns a motorbike, TV and bed. He has no inside toilet or even running water. I wanted to renovate the place for him but he doesn't want that. He tells me that his second room is for me. He says: "I know you have money now, but the room is for you if you need it one day".'

As well as being successful in their business ventures, Philippe and Hang have also enjoyed the benefits of the real estate boom in Hanoi. With the profit from their first business they bought a block of land near the Ho Chi Minh Mausoleum and had started to design a house to build when its value almost doubled in a boom market. 'I told my wife we didn't need to build a house on such an expensive block of land.' And anyway, Philippe's preference was to have a bit more space and some trees around him. He started looking in the suburbs and found 600 square metres of land in a village past Gia Lam, across the other side of the Red River. Because it was about 10 kilometres from the centre of Hanoi it was cheap, only a little more than US$30 a square metre. Because of the cheapness of the land, Philippe was able to afford to build a very large and beautiful two-storey house.

Soon other people started getting the idea that life in the suburbs wasn't such a bad thing. Philippe found himself the beneficiary of a land price boom in that area, the value of his land sky-rocketing to more than thirty times what he had paid only three years earlier. Suddenly, he was sitting on a comfortable retirement fund. 'I didn't do it for profit. I feel a bit uncomfortable about it because there is no morality in it. I am happy but I recognise that it's not fair. I never had such money before. I couldn't imagine coming to a communist country to become rich!'

Philippe was enjoying the bucolic pleasures of what Hanoians think of as the countryside and therefore backward and primitive. He planned to build a swimming pool to complete his estate but his wife was unhappy. Even though they had a car she felt she was living too far from Hanoi. They rented a small flat in the centre of Hanoi for a year. When it became clear to Philippe that they weren't likely to go back to living permanently in his dream house, he decided they should rent something nicer in town, at least with a garden, somewhere for his sons to play.

Philippe and Hang had their first child in March 2001 and the second in October 2003. 'Most people get married in their twenties and have children, so then they have less choice in what they can do. I chose another way. Although it wasn't really a deliberate choice, just following my feelings or instinct. Maybe I'm a primitive, but doing things this way has never brought unhappiness and it makes life beautiful. My parents are astonished and happy at becoming grandparents.

My father is eighty-two years old and can't travel to Vietnam. My mother learnt to email at eighty. I visit them in France for a month each year. In August 2003 my wife was pregnant with our second child and I took my son to France with me. After one month he was speaking French.'

Although Hanoi feels very much like home to Philippe these days, in some ways he feels as if he is still travelling. 'I am still looking at everything. It will never be my real country, but I love this country and these people. I love how clever they can be, the little things, the way the street sellers display their wares, how ingeniously they can arrange their goods for display on a bicycle, the details of life, the songs of the sellers in the streets. I never get tired of it.'

The language creates a bit of a barrier for Philippe and he finds pronunciation difficult when trying to speak Vietnamese, with its six different tones. 'I can speak French, Spanish or English. I even learnt Indonesian without much effort, just by living there a long time. I hope the same will eventually happen with Vietnamese. When I try to speak Vietnamese to my family they say they don't understand me, then laugh and don't listen carefully or try to help me. I manage much better when I speak to people in the street. My three-year old son teaches me now and he said to me, "You speak Vietnamese very well, Papa, you have to trust yourself." In fact I don't mind being amongst Vietnamese and not understanding. I like to be alone and that way I am alone but with people.'

Friends are still very important to Philippe and some of his oldest friends now live in Hanoi. Ali, his friend from university days, opened a restaurant next door to Philippe's first shop after some urging and is now happily settled in Hanoi. His old friend, the other Philippe, was planning to live in Australia and had already obtained his business visa, but on the way called in to spend Christmas in Hanoi with his friends. After a while he decided that Australia was too organised and that the chaos of Vietnam suited him better. So now he and Philippe have opened two stores in Hanoi that import French clothing for the Vietnamese market.

There is quite a large French community in Hanoi, maybe around one thousand people these days, many attached to the Embassy or business organisations, but others like Philippe and his friends, who came by themselves and found something to do. A small group of Philippe's friends are planning to buy some land on the coast a few hours' drive from Hanoi and erect some traditional wooden houses there so they can go away together for holidays. Maybe this plan reminds Philippe of his days of communal living in the south of France. He still keeps the small house that he bought there thirty years ago and visits when he goes to France. His first wife, who went on to marry a doctor and have three children, is a neighbour and remains a friend. 'I don't like people who hate others, or themselves. I once wrote a song about it. People can separate but still like each other. You don't spit on your past love, otherwise it is like cancelling your own story, your own past. It might be the end of that story, but you can still like each other.'

Philippe certainly doesn't regret not becoming a journalist, but he holds nostalgic feelings for his music days. He is disappointed and frustrated that his musical career never went further. His CD was played often on the radio and is still available on the Internet, but for complicated reasons it was never released for sale in stores. When he came to Hanoi he wanted to make a break with music. 'Once I had children I felt no need to write anymore. Perhaps the need to write poetry and to have kids comes from the same urge to create something that lasts longer than you do.' There have been other changes in Philippe's life. 'I don't need to go out in the evening so much anymore. My wife likes me to be at home. Once I used to stay out until 3 a.m. or 4 a.m. Now I go to bed about 10.30 p.m. and wake up early to play with my kids. Some of my friends are surprised, but I am healthier for it.'

Life in Hanoi is comfortable for Philippe. 'In some ways it can be very difficult to do things here and in other ways very easy. When an opportunity comes you have to decide fast. When you live in a new country you have to be open to change and not be stubborn.' No doubt marriage and children have had an impact, too. 'Before I had no money and spent all of it. Now my wife takes care of the money, she collects it from the shops and saves it. She gives me pocket money. If we go out to eat in a restaurant she pays because I don't have any money. Now I am rich but I still don't have any money!'

According to the Vietnamese lunar calendar, Philippe is a Buffalo, and in the western zodiac, a bull. Maybe, after a rampaging youth of travel, women and song, this mellowing bull has found his green pastures and is ready to enjoy this new phase of family life. 'I love my life. You don't have to be rich or very clever or very beautiful but you can still have a fabulous adventure!'

Carla's Story:
For the Love of a Sailor

Carla initially thought that when she met and fell in love with a sailor that they would sail the world together, travelling from one exotic port to another. Little did she imagine that she would spend the next decade in the land-locked city of Hanoi, eventually running an Italian restaurant and raising two daughters there. An adventure of course, just not the one she expected.

Carla was born in 1964 into an upper middle-class family living in the small town of Osimo near the Adriatic Coast, in Italy. Her father was a doctor, but her mother had given up her job as secretary of a school once she married, as was usual in those times. Carla had a brother who was four years older, and a nanny who cooked and cared for her like a second mother. To this day her nanny still lives with her parents. Carla describes herself as a 'wimpy' child. 'My brother would sometimes hit and shake me and I would always be crying. I was Mum's darling and Dad's little girl.'

Nevertheless, Carla left her loving family when she was fourteen to go to boarding school. This was considered quite adventurous and brave as no-one in her town had ever done that before, although later other girls followed her example. 'I wanted to study languages and the nearest good school for doing that was 50 kilometres away. I still remember my first night alone there. I called my dad and said, "I don't want to be here, I want to come back home." He told me to try it for six months because it was my decision to go there and so I decided to stay and enjoyed it. After high school, I went even further away, 300 kilometres to Florence, where I studied for three years to become an interpreter and translator.'

Carla's father would have loved her to become a doctor, but she didn't have the stomach for it and couldn't see herself performing operations. Instead, she focused on languages, but only the European languages of English, German and French. 'I get along well with Anglo-Saxons and love English as a language. When I visited England I loved the Cotswolds; it felt like going back to something familiar, so I have this thing in my mind that I must have been English in a previous life. I had never thought about Asia and Asian culture. That had been completely out of my picture.'

After becoming qualified, Carla sought employment as an interpreter or translator, but found it hard to break into that small select group without any experience of living abroad. Her next option was to find work with a travel agency. As a tour leader Carla travelled a lot but saw little, being too busy looking after the tour group.

As well as being more adventurous than other girls she knew, Carla was also a romantic. 'Love and romance have always been a big part of my life. I first fell in love at six years of age. At fifteen I had my first serious relationship that lasted four years. I had many boyfriends and was always falling deeply and madly in love!' As a child, Carla had sailed with her family, but after she turned eighteen she refused to go with them anymore. Ten years later she met Leo, a handsome Italian sailor and the love of her life, and started sailing again. 'It was hard for my father to accept that I wanted to marry a sailor and sail around the world with him. But I was madly in love and would have followed him to the South Pole!' When Carla's mother realised that Carla was going to go ahead no matter what they said, she advised her husband that he would have to accept things. She told him, 'At Leo's house they love our daughter and are nice to her. If we keep having this attitude we are going to create a distance between us because we know how stubborn she is once she makes up her mind. She will go for it no matter what we do.' Carla's father asked, 'Does that mean I have to smile and sit back and relax?' Her mother was adamant. 'Exactly,' she replied. This changed the atmosphere and was helped along by the fact that Leo found himself a permanent job instead of the seasonal work he was doing as a boat skipper. Leo started work with two Italian brothers who had come to Vietnam in 1990 and begun a small trading company. They decided they could successfully manufacture paragliders in Vietnam and sell them to the European market where they were all the rage. Because Leo had experience making sails, he was hired on an eighteen-month contract to manage the manufacture of paraglider sails. This allayed some of the fears of Carla's parents; at least they knew where Carla would be for eighteen months and that they would have an income.

Leo had dreamt about sailing since he was six years old. He did his military service in the navy and when Carla met him, was transport-ing sailing boats in the Mediterranean. Taking the job in Vietnam was a compromise for Leo, but the plan was to earn enough money so that they could buy a boat and sail the world. Even though she was twenty-nine when she got married, Carla was concerned about her parents' reaction and wanted their approval for the marriage and so everyone was satisfied when this job turned up.

There was nothing about Vietnam itself that attracted Carla or Leo. They ended up there because Leo found work and that allowed them to get married with Carla's family's blessing. And Carla was ready for a change in her life. 'Because I had already travelled quite a bit, the prospect of going to Vietnam didn't worry me. Italians often cling to their families, but I left home at fourteen so it was easier for me.' Carla gave up her job as a travel agent after a whirlwind courtship of ten months. She and Leo were married in October 1994, had a honeymoon in Spain for two weeks and on 1 November 1994 they flew to Hanoi.

When Carla and her new husband arrived at Noi Bai Airport, ready to begin their new life, they were dismayed to find there was no-one to pick them up. They had no name or telephone number to contact, no address of where they were supposed to be staying, nothing to help them. In 1994 the airport in Hanoi was a small, cheerless building with no facilities for travellers and no proper airport taxis either.

Carla and Leo, tired and disoriented after a long flight, walked out of the airport building into a huge mob of people all shouting and vying for their business, offering to drive them to town. Not knowing what to do, they waited and waited in the hope that someone would turn up to meet them. But as the last passenger headed off and the airport closed up for the night, they had little choice but to hire the last remaining driver who had waited patiently for this chance.

But where should they tell him to take them? Fortunately, Carla's travel experience came to their aid. Passing through customs she had noticed a large sign advertising the Sofitel Metropole Hotel in Hanoi and recognised it as belonging to an international chain. So they instructed their driver to take them there, not realising they had picked the most exclusive and expensive place in the city at that time.

Relieved to be out of the airport at least, they headed for the city, on the way passing two men and three pigs on a motorbike. 'There was one pig lying between the driver and pillion passenger. The other two pigs were tied on either side so that the passenger had his legs over them both. I said to Leo, "Well, this is going to be an interesting country!" '

After being overcharged by their driver they arrived at the Metropole only to find it was fully booked. However, the manager advised them to wait another thirty minutes. If the Japanese people who had booked a room didn't turn up they could have their booking for the night. Luckily, they got the room and then spent a huge amount of money ringing Italy to find out why there was no-one to meet them and where they were meant to be.

'Apparently there had been a mix-up with dates and they were expecting us the day after. The next morning, Leo's boss came to pick us up from the lobby of the Metropole to take us to the place we were supposed to be—a room in a guesthouse for US$10 a night, in the overcrowded old quarter of the city. That first day Leo went to work I looked down from the tiny balcony and thought, I'm not going down there! I stayed in the room all day. It was another world!'

Carla was fascinated with watching the traffic from her balcony, especially at the intersection. It was like an elaborate dance of cars, trucks, motorbikes, bicycles, pedestrians and sometimes livestock weaving past each other. She learnt how to cross the road. 'Just keep a steady pace going straight ahead, one foot after the other, don't look to the right or left, never show any uncertainty or you're dead. It took me quite a while to learn that.'

On the second day, Carla tried going out of the room. Foreigners were still seen as quite a novelty. Children and street-sellers or other people wanting to practice English or catch her attention pursued her or called out to her constantly, making it hard to enjoy a walk. After two weeks, the mother of the girlfriend of Leo's boss rented a house for them and Carla busied herself setting up home, going to the market to buy food and exploring the city. Soon, she become used to the traffic and was riding a bicycle everywhere. 'The traffic wasn't as bad as it is now and there was less pollution. These days you can hardly breathe when riding.' She also got used to dealing with Vietnamese, bargaining with *cyclo* drivers and market-sellers, learning to communicate without much language with varying degrees of success.

Not long after arriving, Carla set off on her bicycle to buy some candles to keep as back-up for the frequent power cuts Hanoi used to experience. She didn't know the Vietnamese word for candle, but thought she would be able to see them in a shop and just point. However, it proved a bit more difficult than she had imagined and eventually she stopped at a pharmacy in the hope that someone might speak English or French. After trying various languages unsuccessfully, Carla resorted to hand gestures, trying to describe a candle shape. At first her audience of Vietnamese men in the shop looked bewildered. Then the light dawned on one man, or so he thought. 'I can still see the look on his face as he raised his hand and with a big grin said, condoms!'

In September 1995, after being in Hanoi for eleven months, Carla headed back to Italy to prepare for her first baby, which was due in November that year. 'There was no international hospital in Hanoi at that time. Earlier in my pregnancy I had an ultrasound examination in a Vietnamese hospital and that was quite an experience. I decided that I wasn't adventurous enough to have the baby in Hanoi.' Since Leo had to get back to work, this meant that Carla had to make the long trip back to Hanoi only twelve days after giving birth. She decided it would be better to make the trip when she had Leo to help carry everything than wait another month and then have to struggle with luggage and a baby alone. It took twelve hours to Bangkok, another one and a half hours to Hanoi and then an hour's drive on rough roads from the airport before they made it home.

Carla employed a young Vietnamese girl to help her with the baby and with the aid of an English–Vietnamese dictionary she learnt to communicate. 'At first it was basic words like food, change nappy, sleep, and slowly I built up my vocabulary. This girl had no experience with foreigners. She was a country girl whose job before had been cooking *pho* (noodle soup), but she had good instincts with the baby. Then suddenly one day, after working for us for two years she said she was moving to Ho Chi Minh City and was catching the bus the next day. After that I found someone who had two children of her own and she worked for me six days a week.'

While Carla was doing battle on the home front, Leo was finding his job more and more difficult. After a two-year struggle of trying to get materials and attend to all the other problems of production in Vietnam, the owners decided to give up the idea. Leo and Carla had already started talking about what she might be able to do, but now they started considering what they both might do. They could go back to Italy, but there was no secure job waiting there. Now that they had a family to consider, the dream of sailing around the world would have to go on hold a bit longer. His past two years' experience had confirmed for Leo that he wasn't made for working for someone else. So that left them to invent something to do that they both enjoyed. Since they were sociable and enjoyed food, they decided to start a real Italian restaurant in Hanoi.

'We saw Vietnam as a pioneer land, a good place to test ourselves. We knew that the expat community understood the problems of operating here and would be more forgiving of our mistakes and it would certainly be easier than trying to open a restaurant in Italy and face the competition of the professionals there. There was almost no competition in Hanoi at the time and we started in a narrow three-storey house in Nguyen Huu Huyen Street in April 1997.' They called their restaurant Mediterraneo, a place that is in Leo's heart and mind at all times.

Very quickly they discovered the limitations of the building they had rented, especially in the heat of summer, and started looking for a new location. The street opposite the Catholic Cathedral has now become one of Hanoi's trendiest, full of a variety of restaurants and cafes and boutiques. But when Leo and Carla were looking for a new place, the only attraction in that area was a new café that was under construction. Nevertheless, they decided the location was good and moved their restaurant to Nha Tho Street in October 1997. Meanwhile, Carla gave birth to their second daughter in September 1997. Clearly the dream of escaping to sail around the world was going to have to be shelved for some time and replaced with the hard work of running a restaurant that opened seven days and nights a week as well as raising two children.

In the early days of the restaurant everything was new to them. First, they had Vietnamese staff, most of whom had never seen or tasted Italian food. Then there was the language barrier. The staff waiting on tables spoke some English, but not those working in the kitchen. Leo and Carla had to extend their Vietnamese vocabulary to include food and cookery terms. Next, there was a search for ingredients. 'Lack of artichokes was a big problem for our cooking. The ones grown here are big but lack flavour. You couldn't get zucchinis here until about 1998, the celery tastes different and there is no parsley, only dill. It was also hard to buy meat left on the bone. We brought over an electric pizza oven from Italy but then had to break the doorway to get it in. Now we will never be able to get it out!'

'We were the first restaurant to introduce homemade fresh pasta. We had never done it before, only watched it being made, so we had to phone home to get help. But Leo is good with his hands and he mastered the technique. Now he is making homemade mozzarella, which is not an easy process! On one trip to Italy he spent two days at a place where it is made, taking photos and making notes. He came back and started practising until he perfected it. The other important aspect of a restaurant is management and we had no experience of that either. How to calculate the quantities of food needed, how to store it, what to do with leftovers.

'At first we would make large quantities of lasagne and freeze the excess, heating it in the microwave before serving. One night a customer who had been recommended by the Italian Embassy called me over and showed me the inside of the lasagne still frozen. Our early customers were like guinea pigs as we learnt how to do things. Sometimes we felt frustrated at our lack of professional training, but we couldn't afford the time to go and learn. Then there were all the other things outside our control, like frequent power cuts in the early days where refrigeration, airconditioning, fans and ovens didn't work, and the cultural misunderstandings with staff.'

Carla and Leo weathered some difficult times, such as the 1998 Asia economic crisis when many foreigners left Hanoi, and then terrorist and SARS scares when tourists stayed away. They moved house several times too, finally finding what they consider the perfect place in Gia Lam, a suburb outside Hanoi across the Red River. 'It was built by a Vietnamese woman married to an Australian man. It is a big house with a garden and small pool with space for two dogs and a cat. Sometimes I like to bicycle to work across the old Long Bien Bridge and I would recommend the experience. There are no cars allowed, only bicycles and sometimes the train. All the vendors with their baskets full of fruit and vegetables and flowers coming to market use it. It is quiet and you can feel the breeze coming from the river and time doesn't exist.'

After six years of working together in the restaurant, Carla and Leo decided it was time for a change and that Carla should think about finding something different to do. As if by design, someone approached Leo about whether he knew anyone or was interested himself in working for Eurocham—the European Chamber of Commerce—that had been established in Hanoi since 1999. It was decided that it would be perfect for Carla and so negotiations and applications went ahead and Carla began work as Director of Eurocham in May 2003. 'It sounded scary at the beginning but after a year I felt confident. The main part of the job is PR, getting to know about the members, running seminars and meetings, providing networking opportunities. It is interesting, especially being the only foreign woman in a group of foreign men, since most of the CEOs and chief representatives of companies are men. I think women are better at the diplomacy that is often needed in these situations. Although we like the idea of being European, in fact there is often not much unity and each keeps his own national characteristics, so I sometimes have to sort out these issues.'

Carla also enjoys the change this new job and routine brings to her family life. 'One of the things I really missed when I was working nights at the restaurant was putting my girls to bed each night. I used to send the girls to school in the morning, go to the restaurant from 11 a.m. to 3 p.m., spend the afternoon with the girls after school and then, at 7 p.m., I had to go back to the restaurant. The nanny would put them to sleep. Now, with this new job, the deal is that I don't have anything to do with running the restaurant anymore. I can read a story to my girls and put them to bed at night. On the other hand, Leo and I have less time together. He is ready to go out after work to relax but I am tired by then. So on the weekends we try to find time together.

'Running a restaurant is a very peculiar way of life. It is crucial to have an Italian running an Italian restaurant. Just the fact of you being there makes people believe the food tastes different. They need to see you there. Sometimes I think that Leo feels lonely and abandoned now that I have this new job. It is good for him not having me around and having to be more social. I feel better having something that is completely mine. I am not sure I could go back to the restaurant now.'

Nor is she sure if they could go back to live in Italy now. 'Italy has become a place we go for holidays now and I am always shocked at the prices there. Vietnam is not so cheap when we take into account school fees for the girls at the international school and trips back to Italy, but we can enjoy a lifestyle here that we could never achieve in

Italy. We have a maid who lives in, a nanny for the girls, a driver for the car. So whenever I feel stressed about living in Vietnam I have to consider all these other things. Hanoi is a place that needs time, you cannot come here and exploit it quickly, but it can also be a good proving ground. The longer we stay here the harder it gets to leave.'

According to Carla, Italian people and Vietnamese people share many similarities. 'First there is the love of noise, in the sense that we are not bothered by it. Then there is the sense of family, a big issue in both societies. Football, of course. Vietnamese fans know all the Italian soccer players and watch all the games on TV. The food in both countries is different but holds the same place of importance in social life. Art is valued and appreciated, especially in the north of both countries. The traffic is crazy in both countries and there is a detachment from politics. Politicians talk and ordinary people ignore it and just get on with their lives without becoming too involved.'

Vietnam opened many new doors for Carla. She learnt about cooking and running a restaurant and has now moved into a new area of international business promotion. Vietnam also opened her eyes to art, something she had no experience of before. 'I hadn't been to an art gallery before, there were no galleries in the town where I lived in Italy, but here they are everywhere. A Swiss woman who became a close friend first showed me around the galleries and I was fascinated.

'Now foreigners have begun to discover Vietnamese artists and I regret that I didn't buy any paintings in the early days when I first came here, but I wasn't into it at that time. Now they are too expensive.' At the Fine Arts College Carla took some lessons in lacquer art, but later discovered she had a passion for drawing and watercolours. Now, her fantasy is to be a retired lady of leisure who indulges her passions for painting and yoga, another interest she took up in Hanoi.

And what of the life lessons learned in Hanoi? 'I have learnt to relax, go at a slower pace, not to get too stressed by time. A Vietnamese once said to me, "You foreigners say that time is money. We Vietnamese are very rich because we have plenty of time." I have also learnt not to get upset when someone smiles at you after they make a mistake, but it is still difficult sometimes. After handling a bicycle, motorbike and car in Hanoi I think that I can drive anywhere in the world, although I have been known to do some terrible things now when I drive in Italy!'

Carla has always enjoyed simple food and so has enjoyed that aspect of living in Vietnam where it is easy to get good simple fresh food. 'Sometimes when working at the restaurant I would order in a Vietnamese meal of rice and meat and vegetables because I was sick of the Italian menu. But I had to hide it so customers didn't see me. I also love soups, and soups in general are very good in Vietnam.'

For the children it has been a great experience, too. 'They live in an international environment. They go to an English-speaking school and speak Italian at home with Leo and me. They have friends at school who are Australian, Dutch and Korean. It is a very safe place. I can send them to a party with their nanny and the driver and know they will be safe. At this age it is perfect for them and they can experience a life they would never get living in Italy.'

When Carla and Leo first came to Hanoi there were only about thirty or forty Italians living in the city, most of them attached to the Italian Embassy. There was a strong sense of community and support. There were also not so many restaurants, and so it was in many ways the pioneer land they expected. 'Although it wasn't inevitable that you would succeed, if you found your niche and worked hard there was a good chance of success.' While being far away from families meant some loss of support, there were advantages. 'We were away from the cares of small family issues, we didn't have to worry about whose family to visit on Sunday, we were left to sort out our own problems, we weren't subjected to disapproval and so it was liberating.'

Instead of a biological family, Carla and Leo found support amongst their expat friends. 'I believe every young couple should have a chance to live abroad. Vietnam is a special place. You hear so many people say that they can't stand the place any more, they are tired of it, have had enough. Then, three or six months later they come back, saying how they missed it so much and so found a job that brought them back. Or they will write emails saying how they can't settle because they are missing Vietnam. There is definitely something about the place that makes it special. We expected to spend two years here and then be off sailing the world. Now we live in a landlocked city with two kids. I have spent a quarter of my life in Hanoi now, so it is a significant experience. No matter where I go from here, this will always remain as one important milestone in my life. It can be a love–hate thing but it gets inside you. In the end it is fascinating; it's a spell. Vietnam is a spell!'

Martin's Story: Sound Advice

Music has always been an important part of Martin's life. Martin was born in Melbourne, Australia, in 1963, the fifth of seven children. He remembers always having music at home and the family singing together, especially on long car trips. Martin's father was the son of a rabbit-trapper cum lift-operator cum department-store Santa. He learnt to play piano on a piece of masonite with the keys painted on, getting to finger a real instrument only once a week at his piano lesson. When his father became a successful lawyer, the family had two pianos for the seven children to play. All Martin's brothers and sisters had piano lessons, but Martin started playing without any tuition, preferring to be left to his own devices. 'Anything I wanted to play that was too difficult I would get my sister to read and watch her play and follow, otherwise I just worked it out for myself.'

Martin attended a Christian Brothers Catholic school where he was often found playing the piano in the school hall instead of sport. He was a clever kid and found schoolwork easy when he was young, but he was lazy and naughty. He took ill with rheumatic fever and scarlet fever together and spent almost a year in bed, at a time when his classmates were learning the foundations of reading and spelling, and he never really caught up on that lost time. But he continued his interest in music throughout his school days, took up the tuba, eventually becoming a State Champion, and played in brass bands and Little Dixie bands.

Towards the end of Year 11 it was suggested that he repeat the year, as his results did not look promising. However, his best mate was planning to study Year 12 at TAFE and so Martin followed him without telling his parents. Unfortunately he didn't have the self-discipline to apply himself to his studies and only passed the music subjects. The next year he was sent back to school where he passed English but not enough other subjects to matriculate and study music at university. 'At this point my parents encouraged me very strongly to join the Army to do music.'

Martin passed the musical audition to enter the defence force music school, but when he went to join the regular army he came up against the army psychologist. The psychologist told me,'"You don't want to be in the army." I insisted that I did but he said, "Believe me, you don't. You know you don't and I know you don't." And he was right, but I argued with him. Eventually he told me to join the Army Reserve for a year and after that to come back.'

Martin joined the Reserve's band where he mostly did practice and drinking and not much army. After only six months he went back to the psychologist who then agreed to transfer him to the regular army. 'I got a hard time during basic training because I'd been in the Reserve and was going into the band. Life was hell and I hated it. But I had known what to expect because my father had been a Reservist until he was fifty and he helped me get through the time. But it was a shock to realise such people existed and that the system fosters them, especially as I had grown up happy and sheltered as a child and had been able to do anything I wanted. The army had to make you blindly obedient and I was not obedient by nature.'

Eventually the hard physical training came to an end and Martin, having signed up for six years, moved to the army band. However, the psychologist turned out to be correct and after two years Martin wanted out. 'The music school was a wonderful experience. It was a brand new college with individual practice rooms and a beautiful fifty-piece band. We got a good education, went to concerts, had guest speakers come and were generally considered musicians rather than soldiers. But just playing tuba was too boring. I was offered saxophone training as an alternative and although I learnt to play in a year I couldn't reach the level required to pass the exam and so I was allowed to leave, with an option to return a year later if I could pass the exam.'

As it turned out there was little chance of that happening. Martin was twenty-two years old by this time and found he could get work easily playing saxophone in bands around Melbourne. Then he headed overseas for about a year, spending time mainly in England and Turkey. He did various casual jobs, but ended up in debt so that once he was back in Australia he knew he would have to find a job.

Kew Cottages is an institution in Melbourne for the intellectually disabled, with about fifteen hundred disabled residents and six hundred psychiatric patients at that time. Martin knew they were always looking for staff and decided to apply for a job as an aide. He found that despite being put in the worst places, often with violent patients, he liked the job.

'I liked the hard work aspect of it, of being really tired and then resting. I didn't get that feeling as a musician. And I liked looking after people and found I could do it easily. My mother, who had worked as a nurse after raising her children, had always said I was a very kind boy and would make a good nurse or kindergarten teacher.' Martin clearly had an aptitude for the work and was offered a place in the hospital's nursing school, the last hospital-based training course in Victoria. He spent more than seven years, from 1986 to

1994, working there. He also managed to keep playing music in bands around Melbourne and because of the shift work, which gave him roughly one month off every three months, he was able to travel a lot.

In 1992 he flew to Ho Chi Minh City on a backpacking holiday. 'I bought a cheap fare via Manila. I found Manila horrible and was ready for the same level of stress when I arrived in Ho Chi Minh City. But it wasn't like Manila at all. It was exciting to see the old American planes and helicopters and buildings as I landed at Saigon airport. And there were beautiful girls and beautiful big trees in the streets. Just on the taxi ride into the city from the airport I felt all the knots come out of my neck and I immediately thought I could live here. I got as far as Hue in central Vietnam, but never made it to Hanoi that trip.'

Martin claims that it was the election of Jeff Kennett as Premier of Victoria that drove him from Australia. A Liberal Party leader committed to economic rationalism, reducing the public service and breaking the unions, Kennett inflamed passions in the State of Victoria. According to Martin, the budget cuts made under Kennett's regime created conditions in his work environment that were dangerous for both clients and staff. In support of his claim, eighteen months after he resigned his position at Kew Cottages there was a fire, and nine of his friends who lived there were burnt to death.

But it wasn't only the political and social climate in Melbourne at the time that was responsible for Martin's cynicism. In high school and later when he was in the army, Martin began to develop his own beliefs and opinions about a wide range of issues. He found himself at odds with his parents and teachers over religion. As he read and travelled more he discovered the wonders of the East—of Angkor Wat, the advanced technology of ancient China, the splendour of non-European civilisations at a time when Europe was still relatively primitive, and realised he had received a totally Eurocentric education. 'My teachers didn't give me a good education at all. They selected what suited their purposes for me to learn. I also began to understand that with religion, people were devoting their lives to believing what is empirically not true. It was a loss of innocence. I am not bitter about it now, but I went through a stage of understanding that the communists were right about many things. I had always been curious about Vietnam. I remember looking through a *Time* magazine where Vietnam featured when I was about eight or nine. I can still remember specific photos of the Vietnam War and seeing it on television every night. I started to have the feeling that the information I had been given on Vietnam was also not the full story. And I was absolutely correct. I am glad I went and had a look for myself. I facetiously say that Jeff Kennett forced me into the arms of the communists, but philosophically it is true.'

After he finished working at Kew Cottages, Martin set off with his girlfriend to travel for one year as he had promised her. The plan was to go to Thailand and spend two months on a beach, then go on to Vietnam for three months with the intention of checking out how he might be able to live there and what he might be able to do. After that they would head to the United States for eight months and tour by combi-van.

In Saigon they bought Minsk motorcycles to drive all the way north to Hanoi, despite the fact that his girlfriend had never ridden a motorbike before. 'I gave her one hour's training and three days later we headed off with our backpacks in the pouring rain. It turned out to be a wonderful, but very difficult trip. I got a bladder infection so it became really uncomfortable riding a motorbike. In Hue it rained for ten days. We had no proper rain gear. We could only buy the cheap Chinese thin plastic coats that ripped and so we were always wet and freezing. The hotels were always tiled and cold and we would have to put our wet clothes back on each day. On the last day on the way to Hanoi it finally stopped raining. I knew immediately when I reached

Hanoi it was the place. By then Saigon was already showing signs of becoming like a little Bangkok.'

After their ordeal, they splurged on a comfortable hotel with plenty of hot water and TV and stayed for two nights. Walking around Hoan Kiem Lake in the centre of Hanoi on their second day, a young man approached them asking if they were looking for somewhere to stay and took them to his friend's house. The owners spoke English, the wife was a haematologist at a big hospital and the husband the director of a scientific laboratory. Martin and his girlfriend rented a room from them for two weeks. During that time, Martin went to the university and found he could obtain a three-month visa if he enrolled in a Vietnamese language course. So after finishing his travels around the United States, and also finishing his relationship with his girlfriend as it happened, Martin headed back to Hanoi to start a new adventure that would, curiously enough, eventually bring him back to his old love of music.

It was 1996 when Martin returned to Hanoi and enrolled in a three-month Vietnamese language course. Every day, between classes, he would scan the English-language national newspaper, *Vietnam News*, looking for work. Whilst checking about a job as an office manager at the Australian Embassy, a position he quickly realised he wasn't qualified for, someone suggested he apply to the newly opened International Medical Clinic nearby.

A few days after presenting himself at the clinic he received a call from a doctor. A Korean woman had tried to commit suicide and they needed someone with psychiatric nursing experience to stay overnight with her at the clinic. That was just the break he needed. By morning the patient was calm and singing his praises and Martin was employed. For Martin it was a dream come true. 'It was a wonderful job, I loved the staff, the patients and I got to travel a lot. The advantage for the clinic in employing a foreign nurse was not only could I communicate better with foreign patients, but I could also accompany medical evacuees, whereas Vietnamese people didn't have the necessary passports and visas.'

One of Martin's duties at the clinic was doing medical checks for students awarded AusAID scholarships to study in Australia. One day, Martin was weighing and measuring a shy little girl and asked her where she was going to study. 'Melbourne,' she told him, 'to study piano'. Just the week before, Martin had been in Melbourne visiting his parents. 'I was playing the piano at home and my mother came into the room crying. When I asked what was wrong she said that the house had two pianos and in the old days there was always someone playing and she had forgotten how much she loved it. So I thought of my mother when this girl said she was studying piano. I asked her if she knew anyone in Australia. When she said no, I told her, "Now you do, you've got a new grandma!"

Martin arranged for this student to stay with his parents and play their piano while she was studying, a mutually beneficial arrangement. Martin's parents now have a network of Vietnamese friends in Australia and when his mother comes to Hanoi for a visit she never has any free time for sightseeing, always heading off to meet someone's family or have a reunion with a returned student.

Martin's job at the clinic also provided the circumstances for meeting his future wife. An American man had broken his leg and was being evacuated to Bangkok under Martin's care. Because he had his leg in a splint, he took up three seats, so Martin couldn't sit with him. Instead, he found himself sitting next to a Vietnamese woman. He realised he had met her briefly through friends who were staying at a hotel owned by the family of this woman's ex-husband. She was working for a Vietnamese Government tourist company now and taking a group of Vietnamese to Bangkok. She said, 'You're Martin aren't you?'

From then on they talked and talked. 'We got on so well that I found her that night at her hotel and we talked some more, and we continued to meet when we returned to Hanoi. It was a very old-fashioned courtship and she was just delightful. We would go out for coffee and she would bring along an interesting clipping from the paper to encourage conversation.' Even though she had been long separated from her husband, her relationship with Martin had to be kept hidden to avoid gossip and criticism until about a year before their marriage in 2002.

In April 1999 Martin finished working at the medical clinic. He took the time to relax and enjoy a break before starting work in November of that year with an international non-governmental organisation (NGO) on a trachoma project. Trachoma is a very contagious eye disease that eventually leads to blindness in a very painful way, scarring the inside of the eyelid and ultimately turning the eyelashes inward, scratching the eyeball. If one person in a close community is infected, the bacteria are transferred easily and everyone gets the disease. In the past it required rigid compliance of twice-daily applications of a tetracycline cream for eight to ten weeks. If anyone missed their treatment for a few days, the bacteria would spread again and the village would never get rid of it. But now there was a new treatment available. With only one dose, the body would be free of the bacteria for a week. This meant if a whole village was treated at the same time, the disease could be completely eradicated as the transmission chain had been broken.

Martin's project adopted a four-pronged approach called SAFE. Surgery to correct the later stages of the disease. Antibiotics to kill the bacteria. Facial hygiene to educate people not to share towels and pillows. Environment that looked at factors like clean water supplies, reducing flies and such.

The job fitted well with Martin's skills and interests: he was a nurse, he spoke Vietnamese and he liked getting out into the countryside. Over three years the project operated in nine districts in seven provinces in North Vietnam with great success. From a beneficiary population of 1.8 million they managed more than one million face-to-face interactions in eighteen months. Later, the Vietnamese Ministry of Health took over the project and extended the reach. At first, Martin really enjoyed the job, but towards the end of the three years it required more time spent in front of a computer and dealing with bureaucracies. He could have stayed on with the organisation but by this time he was suffering more and more from intestinal problems, partly caused by the stress of the job he believes.

In October 2002 Martin went to Bangkok for surgery to remove part of his colon to treat his diverticulitis. Before this time Martin and Ly had decided to get married, although Martin says it really wasn't a 'decision' but more of a natural symbiosis because they got on so well. While Martin was recuperating from his operation on a beach in Thailand, their marriage papers came through from the Vietnamese Department of Justice. Although their official marriage date is recorded in November 2002, the day they collected their papers in Hanoi, they had a series of parties with families and friends in 2003 to celebrate. Martin's parents, five of his siblings and some friends came to Hanoi to celebrate the marriage. The group all gathered at a friend's house and walked a short way to Ly's sister's house in the afternoon.

'We didn't want a traditional wedding, because that isn't who we are and we didn't want to make it like a tourist show. I knew if it was natural it would be delightful enough and walking together to the bride's family home had an element of a traditional village wedding that was nice.' There were no prayers, no ceremony, no vows, and no answering to anyone, which satisfied Martin's anti-religious stance. But he did pay his respects to Ly's late father at the family altar and promised that he would take good care of his daughter. And he did wear a suit and his wife a traditional red Vietnamese wedding *ao dai*.

Once they had decided to marry, Ly left her job with the Vietnamese tourist company and shortly after, with Martin's encouragement, she and her friend started their own small in-bound tourist company. At one point Martin had toyed with the idea of studying a Master of Public Health degree in Bangkok to help him find a better job in Hanoi. However, when the SARS scare was on, his wife's travel business wasn't doing so well and he didn't want to use up his savings on course fees. He applied for a few jobs unsuccessfully and eventually realised that he probably wasn't going to find a job unless it was one he didn't like. It was at this point that Martin decided to turn a potential difficulty into an opportunity.

Martin had always managed to play some music since he arrived in Hanoi. There were various expat bands around that were fluid in composition as people came and went and while they occasionally played in public, they enjoyed practising together more than performing. Some good Vietnamese musicians were also involved, but in those days they were so poor that the foreigners would pay them to come to rehearsal out of their own pockets. 'Our music cost us money instead of making us any money at that time. These days some of those Vietnamese players have their own TV shows or perform regularly on TV and in orchestras, they are well travelled and earn more money that I do now!' Martin realised that without a job he would have time to devote himself to his music. 'For a long time I had had this idea of a group with three Vietnamese girl singers, and so it seemed like now was the time to try it.' Martin found his three Vietnamese female singers. He also found three Vietnamese men to play electric guitar, bass guitar and drums. One foreigner was found to play the acoustic guitar and another to play harmonica. Martin played keyboard and sometimes guitar. He called his group Sound Advice, a play on words and reference to the role he plays amongst his friends of providing comfort and advice when needed. His group has an eclectic repertoire ranging from schmalz to country, blues and toe-tapping oldies. There is also a bit of tongue-in-cheek when the Vietnamese girls are singing the old Andrews Sisters song, 'Rum and Coca-Cola', about 'working for the Yankee dollar'.

So far there are not enough bookings to support the group. The music scene in Hanoi is undeveloped with only a few places like the Press Club with its regular expat gatherings every Friday evening, and the Met Pub, a popular watering hole for foreigners prepared to pay for professional bands. But mostly, Martin wanted to raise the standards of the bands playing for foreign audiences and to participate in developing a vital quality music scene.

As far as making money is concerned, he only has small needs. He teaches piano and guitar to some foreign children and has the potential to expand this work. 'In Vietnamese society, to be a music teacher is a noble thing to do and that resonates with my beliefs. If you are not engaged in a struggle to bring down evil empires and save the world, then you have to find other noble things to do like teaching children and caring for your family.' Martin helps out sometimes in his wife's travel business and recognises that she has better earning capacity than he does. They are both happy for him to care for their daughter, who was born in January 2004. 'Time spent with my daughter is worth more than anything anyone could offer me at this stage.'

Happiness is important to Martin and he has learnt some valuable lessons in Vietnam. 'I am convinced that Vietnamese people are happier than Australian people. You only need to spend ten minutes at the airport here and spend ten minutes at the airport in Australia to see that. Rich people in Hanoi are not happier than poor farmers in the countryside. Maybe they are less happy. Although life is hard, happiness is a basic condition for Vietnamese. They are happy if nothing is going wrong. If something is going wrong they can still be happy because they expected it to go wrong. For westerners, no matter how good life is, we are always pushing ahead, looking for the next promotion or a better car. Happiness is something we are always striving for, not something we have now. Vietnamese get happiness from their family, from the taste of food, from simple things, solid pleasures.' These days Martin gets his pleasure from taking care of his daughter, riding his Minsk motorbike out in the countryside to take photos, swimming and watching the world go by on the streets of Hanoi, either alone or over a beer with friends.

Vietnam has provided some important lessons too. 'Vietnamese are fatalistic: life is hard, we do the best we can and hope it's better next time. I have come to realise it isn't necessary to understand everything so why torture yourself trying. This is a big change for me. Before I was always trying to find answers, now I understand less but I'm relaxed about it. After living here, I realise there are other ways of seeing, what I call "the third way". If I give my wife a problem to solve she comes up with an answer I can understand but would never have thought of myself. It is logical but not my logic. So there are complete dimensions missing in my western way of seeing. It is like a Chinese scroll painting that can be unrolled in either direction to reveal different parts of the picture, unlike a defined framed piece of western art.

'I have also come to understand much more about my parents, especially my father, and I have some new and different warm feelings towards them now. When the Vietnam War ended I was the same age as my father had been at the end of the Second World War. My father used to talk about how, as a kid, he remembered seeing lots of maimed and limbless people after the end of the war. In Vietnam I have seen the same. My father's generation was told to fight for their country. I am in Asia because Gough Whitlam, Bob Hawke and Paul Keating [Australian Prime Ministers in the 1970s and 1980s] told my generation we should engage with our near northern neighbours. I saw the Vietnam War on TV every night. My father knew people who had been tortured by the Japanese. Coming to Vietnam allowed me to step away and understand more about my father and myself and see our common ground.'

Learning a language is another pleasure Martin has enjoyed. After the initial three months of lessons when he first arrived, he spent another three months when he finished working at the medical centre to consolidate his knowledge. These days he says that he and his wife speak a sort of 'Vinglish' where they select the shortest word in either language. But he enjoys the way that learning a new language forces you to think about the meaning of each word and its origins. In Vietnam the language is still closely associated with its origin, with many words derived from a rural life that still continues much the same as centuries ago. Understanding Vietnamese also opens up so much more of the society and Martin enjoys striking up conversations with strangers and listening to their stories. He sees it as a quest to collect pieces of the mosaic of life that will perhaps take shape and make sense just before he dies.

Martin believes in letting the future take care of itself. He thinks that people are most valuable when they are doing something they like, such as playing music. He says that maybe one day he will find a more meaningful pursuit in his life, like working in an orphanage in Hanoi, or helping couples adopt Vietnamese babies. Or maybe he will study psychology and find a way to combine it with the insights he has gained by living in Vietnam. But he is not fretting about it for now. 'I am happy in my life. My life with my wife is beautiful and she challenges me intellectually. At present, when I wake up every morning I can say: everything I have to do today I like!'

John's Story:
Every Picture Tells a Story

John is a knockabout sort of bloke whose first experience of Vietnam, like many of his generation, was as a twenty-year-old soldier. But, unlike a lot of his fellow soldiers, John claims he had a good war, enjoyed his time in Saigon and fell in love with the country and the people.

Born in London in February 1944, John spent only six months at school in England before his parents took advantage of the post-World War II assisted migration scheme and left the UK for Australia. His earliest memories in Australia are of living in a large old army tent in a camping ground, the Queensland immigration centre, and eventually life in suburban Brisbane.

A bout of encephalitis just before his fourteenth birthday meant he missed the start of the new school year and when he did return he remembers being thrust into an algebra class. This was more than John wanted to cope with and caused him to declare that since he was now fourteen years old he didn't have to stay at school and so he headed for the bush and worked as a jackaroo, a drover, a ringer, and anything else that was going. When he felt like a taste of city life, he would come back to Brisbane and work as a shoe salesman or a storeman at Coles.

In those days it was easy to pick up work. He had been helping his father as a painter since he was twelve years old and so would sometimes return to that as well.

By 1961, when John was seventeen, he had had enough of life in the bush and wanted some more excitement and adventure out of life. He knew he couldn't handle a regular nine-to-five city job. He was in top physical condition, able to run a mile in only a few seconds more than John Landy's record-breaking feat, and could 'shoot the eye out of an eagle' after his years in the bush. It is no surprise then that he would apply and be quickly accepted by the army. 'Infantry for you son', they told him at the recruiting centre.

John signed up for six years of army life and while he claims he was a good soldier he wasn't always an obedient or well-behaved one. In fact, he marvels at the fact that he wasn't actually court-martialled and discharged after taking off for three months following a fist-fight with his sergeant. Instead he only received a small fine after eventually giving himself up to police. He was moved around to different army bases and was mainly involved in transport units or air dispatch. When the Malaysian conflict arose he wasn't allowed to go with his battalion as he wasn't yet nineteen, so he became part of a jungle warfare training team. But by the time the first contingent of Australian soldiers was sent to the Vietnam conflict John was old enough to go, leaving behind his wife and son and, some months later, a daughter.

His air-dispatch training resulted in him being attached to the US troops, loading helicopters. After a month he had developed severe tinnitus and was evacuated. However, John's desire for adventure had not been satisfied by this short stint. He wasn't ready to go back to Australia yet and so a driving job was found for him. He spent the next eleven months of his tour of duty ensconced in a hotel in Saigon with maid service, becoming, in his words, 'a sort of Milo Minderbinder' of Catch-22 fame, wheeling and dealing in the black market of Saigon.

When his year of service was up, he tried to stay in Saigon. He was enjoying life to the full and had fallen in love with Lan, the secretary of Air Vice-Marshal Ky. Lan was a chaste young Vietnamese woman whom he could only meet chaperoned. However, he was advised that he must go back to Brisbane, Australia, where he served out the remaining years of his service contract, plus the three months he had been absent.

In early 1968 John was twenty-three years old, still married with two children, and out of the army. He was looking for a job with no idea of ever seeing Vietnam again. After six years of army life the only thing he was sure of was that he didn't ever want to work for a boss again. He tried a bread run, but when he looked like going broke after only six months because his customers couldn't afford to pay their bills, he gave that away and went back to painting; not working for his father, but as a subcontractor with his own team of men.

Then, at thirty-four, John was diagnosed with emphysema and thought he was going to die. His lungs kept collapsing if he tried to work and so by the time he was thirty-six he had to give up work and go on a disability pension. Amidst this turmoil of poor health and loss of work, John's marriage ran aground.

For the next decade John played with the idea of prospecting. First it was dredging for gold until this practice became illegal. Then he tried mining sapphires, and every winter for a number of years would head off to a places like Anakie and Emerald in Victoria where he lived in an old insulated truck body. During this period he had a new partner whom he ultimately married, but despite many years of living harmoniously together before marriage, soon after the marriage took place John found himself unhappy in the relationship.

By 1993, having extricated himself from his second marriage, John was living on Queensland's Gold Coast in a new relationship with a woman he had long known and 'lusted after', who was now separated. In the years intervening since his wartime experience in Vietnam,

John had never had any thoughts of returning to Vietnam. As a young man with family responsibilities he had no opportunity and later when he became too ill to work he didn't have enough money to consider travel.

Then one day in 1998 his partner noticed an ad for a librarian to work in Hanoi on an AusAID-funded education project. She applied, was selected, gave up her job as college librarian and headed off to Vietnam with John as her accompanying partner. Originally the contract period was for two years but was then extended. As far as John is concerned, after five years in Hanoi he never wants to leave Vietnam again.

Hanoi seems to be one of those places where people can reinvent themselves in surprising ways. Maybe it's the fact of being a foreigner in a very different culture with few connections or responsibilities to inhibit you, or the fact that Vietnamese are particularly tolerant of foreigners and their often strange ways that gives people the courage to try things never previously considered.

If you met John for the first time you are wouldn't be surprised to learn he had spent years in the Australian outback prospecting for gold and gemstones. Or even that he and a friend had once tried to build a gyrocopter, running out of time and enthusiasm before getting it off the ground.[9] He looks the type of bloke who would do that! But you might be surprised to learn that soon after arriving in Hanoi, John took up lacquer art and discovered a talent, even holding an exhibition of his work. According to John, it was his partner Gail who encouraged him to try this traditional Vietnamese art 'to keep him out of the bars and away from the local women'. But Gail adds that she thought it was a craft that would suit his perfectionist temperament as well as giving him an interest. And she was right.

The first step was to find a teacher, always easy in Hanoi where it seems possible to find a 'famous' teacher for just about anything you can imagine. That's where John's new friend Thanh came into the picture. Thanh is a savvy young lawyer, typical of the smart, rising younger generation in Hanoi. He's well educated, speaks English, and is eager to soak up everything he can from foreigners and 'integrate into the world'. In addition to opening his own law firm where he employs four full-time lawyers and other collaborators, Thanh opened an art gallery in 1998 in what has recently become a busy up-market tourist area near the Catholic Cathedral in the centre of Hanoi. Thanh explains that his 'right-hand side is the law' but his 'left-hand side is the gallery' and this helps him to 'keep balanced'. 'My gallery allows me to make connections and make friends. I want to help foreigners better understand Vietnam. I tell my staff to treat clients as a friend, not trying to only sell to them. That's my philosophy!'

Thanh met Gail when he was studying a special course of English for lawyers at the centre where she works. Through Gail he met John and the three of them shared a common interest in art. But the friendship between John and Thanh developed beyond art. In fact, Thanh features strongly in all John's activities in Hanoi. It was Thanh who introduced him to an art teacher, Thanh who helped him on his prospecting and jeep-purchasing missions, and Thanh who, even now, helps with advice on exporting Vietnamese products. 'We are friends so we have no border', says Thanh. 'I like so much about John and his character. He is a real man. He speaks straight and is very open. I know he loves Hanoi so much and he understands about Vietnamese people. We enjoy everything together, art, travelling, drinking, talking … everything. In his mind John is young, I love that!'

When John and Gail asked Thanh about finding a lacquer art teacher, Thanh was a little surprised at first to learn that someone of

John's age wanted to take up something new. But then he began to understand more about John. 'When I go with John I seem to get younger,' mused Thanh, nearly thirty years John's junior. 'I want to learn from John and I want to help him become successful because we are friends. When John is successful, Gail will be happy and I will be happy, too.' Thanh's connections with local artists meant he was able to introduce John to Hoan, reputedly one of the best lacquer art technicians in the country, who was also able to speak a little English. Hoan had already taken on a Japanese student and John became his second foreign student.

Traditional Vietnamese lacquer art is a slow and painstaking process of building up layer upon layer of lacquer to create a rich depth of colour and shadow causing a three-dimensional effect. The lacquer used is made from the sap of any of six species of trees from the Anacardiaceae family found in the north and south of Vietnam. Harvested in the same way as rubber, by making an incision in the tree and letting the sap flow, fresh lacquer is initially a whitish colour that turns brown on exposure to air. When it solidifies, it becomes resistant to acid and acts as an ideal protection for wood and bamboo. Lacquered items have been found in ancient tombs in Vietnam dating back to the third and fourth centuries BC. By the eighteenth century, a guild of lacquer specialists had formed in Hanoi. But it was the influence of the French and the establishment of the Fine Arts University in Hanoi in 1925 that saw the techniques that had previously been used for handicrafts and furniture applied to painting to create a new art form.

These days, the best quality lacquer art uses imported Japanese marine ply as the base, thick enough to prevent warping and properly dried to avoid cracking and splitting. Once the board has been cut to the required size and sanded smooth, the first coat of raw lacquer is applied and then covered with gauze on both sides, completely sealing and waterproofing the board. Depending on the technique used and the quality and effect the artist is seeking, as many as fifteen layers of lacquer are applied, drying and sanding between each coat. To obtain the traditional browns, yellows and reds, various clays are added to the lacquer. Each colour has to be applied separately and dried before another colour can be added. The addition of eggshell is a technique commonly used in traditional lacquer art to provide white or cream textured highlights, perhaps picking out a conical hat, or a shirt, or piece of jewellery in the design.

Like many of the best Vietnamese lacquer artists, John buys his boards already prepared. 'It requires a particular skill of its own and I prefer to spend my time on the more creative aspects. But I do prepare my own eggshells!' Hen's eggs can be used but duck eggs are slightly thicker and have a better structure. Once the shell is collected, John puts the pieces into boiling water to make it easier to remove all the inner membrane, and then he gets rid of all the moisture by cooking briefly in a frying pan. Once the board and eggshells are ready, an outline of the picture is traced onto the surface of the board using chalk, marking any sections to be filled with eggshell first. John uses photographs or traced drawings, which is why he refers to it as a craft rather than an art, and to himself as an artisan rather than an artist, but there are some artists using the form for original works, too.

Next comes the delicate step of gouging through layers of lacquer the depth of an eggshell, and then painting the area with lacquer before carefully placing the pieces of eggshell in position and hitting them with a special hammer to break up and spread the pieces evenly. Then comes more smoothing and more lacquering. Once all the eggshell sections have been completed, the rest of the outline is traced onto the board and individual colours are applied layer by layer, drying carefully between each coat. Once the final layer has been applied and dried, it is carefully sanded so that the image and its final deep lustre is revealed.

One false move at any stage, or too vigorous a final sanding for example, can potentially ruin a work. Sometimes pearl shell is used instead of eggshell and this can be more difficult to work with as it is thicker and uneven. Silver leaf can also be used underneath the colours to add depth and lustre, often on a face, and gold leaf can be added as a final touch to add highlights, and sometimes a signature.

While John adheres to the traditional techniques of lacquer art, not all his subjects are traditional Vietnamese ones. He has painted some distinctive Australian subjects, like a kangaroo, a koala, and a possum. He has also painted a very cute gecko, a brightly coloured tree frog and a magnificent squid on a coral reef, a work that took him three months to complete. For a friend who was a fan of the music group The Grateful Dead he copied an album cover with roses entwined through a skeleton. 'Over the years I would have worked on about seventy paintings, but if I wasn't fussed with the result, then I'd just fill it in with lacquer, turn it over and start again on the other side.' Nevertheless, by late 2001 John had produced enough high quality works to hold an exhibition at one of Hanoi's five-star hotels. Australia's then Ambassador to Vietnam, Michael Mann, opened it.

According to John, you never stop learning about lacquer painting. 'Even Hoan, my teacher, who has been painting for fifteen years and whom I consider one of the best technicians working in this field, is still learning. But he has an ability to add a touch of magic to a work that brings it alive.' One of John's works of which he is justifiably proud is of an old Vietnamese man in a conical hat, and he acknowledges that Hoan's 'finessing', just an extra touch of shadow on a cheekbone and a swirl on an eyebrow, brought an added dimension.

For more than three years, John continued going to Hoan's studio almost every morning from 8.30 a.m. until lunchtime, sometimes working on two or three paintings to make use of the time while sections were drying between coats. Then, not long after his successful exhibition where he sold several works, he gave up painting. 'I needed to keep returning to Australia regularly and this began to interfere with the rhythm and continuity of my painting. It wasn't doing my lungs much good either.' Lacquer is a skin irritant causing dermatitis, and has poisonous fumes that are potentially carcinogenic. A few of his unfinished paintings he handed on to Hoan to complete, but as far as John was concerned his lacquer art days had come to an end.

Meanwhile, he had been exploring some other very different areas of activity and so when he stopped painting he had more time for some of these new ventures. One of them harkened back to his earlier interest in metal detecting. 'Not long before I came to Hanoi, I had bought a newfangled metal detector that cost bucket-loads of money, planning to use it in outback Australia. I started thinking that maybe I could put it to good use in Vietnam and so I brought it with me. I went to the mining museum in Hanoi and to some of the gold mining areas to see what sort of gold was there. I had the idea that I could go to some of the ethnic minority areas and help them find gold.' This wasn't to be a money-making exercise for John; the satisfaction was to find gold and help the ethnic people supplement their meagre incomes. If it was a successful means of finding metals, John believed these communities could afford to purchase a communal detector of their own.

With his friend Thanh to help him, John set off for Quang Binh province. But despite the fact that this was where Thanh's father was born and where he still had relatives living, they ran foul of the red tape and bureaucracy and the sensitivities involved in such an enterprise. So John ended up taking his metal detector back to Australia in disgust and disappointment.

However, failed projects have never deterred John. Spurred on again by his friend Thanh, John's next venture involved buying an old jeep. The place to buy a jeep in Vietnam is of course Da Nang, where the United States had a large military base during the Vietnam

War and where there are still vast stocks of spare parts to service these now aging vehicles. Deciding to turn the purchase into a road-trip adventure holiday, John headed off with his partner Gail, Thanh and Thanh's friend Manh, also a lawyer, by plane to Da Nang. There they made contact with Thanh's uncle, a military doctor, who helped them with the purchase of a jeep said to have been owned by the head of military security in Da Nang.

'I thought this would mean it was in reasonable condition and reliable,' said John, 'but just to make sure we had it checked by a local mechanic. In the mechanic's garage, Gail and I were amazed to see a jet ski with "Gold Coast Jet Ski" painted on it. Apparently some Australian guy who was working in Da Nang bought it there and gave it to the mechanic when he left. In retrospect, I would have been better off buying the jet ski from him and bringing that to Hanoi instead of the jeep!' John lamented.

With the purchase completed, the four headed back to Hanoi along Highway One in their newly acquired vehicle, discovering fairly quickly that jeep travel is not the most comfortable means of transportation. When it is dry the dust blows inside and when it is raining everyone gets wet. As it happened, Highway One was being upgraded between Da Nang and Vinh, which meant driving on dirt for half of the journey. But then it rained. 'Whenever anything came driving the other way it would throw up a spray of mud. I could see it coming and duck to miss the worst, but Gail in the back seat,would take the full impact. The jeep was full of slimy yellow mud and when we stopped at a hotel for the night, Gail had to have the mud hosed off her before they would let her inside and she ended up having to throw away those clothes!'

John and Gail settled back into life in Hanoi and recovered from their three-day road trip. John decided, with encouragement from Thanh, that he could make some money by offering tours in his authentic US Army jeep. Anh John's Jeep Tours was born, advertising 'personalised tours of Hanoi in a liberated US jeep with Australian expatriate owner-driver'. However, despite the careful selection and precaution of having it checked by a mechanic, the jeep proved extremely unreliable. 'Every time it got a tourist in it, the thing would die,' complained John. 'And it was expensive to run as it had an old-fashioned engine. So, by the time I took into account the repair costs as well as running costs, I couldn't compete with Vietnamese tour drivers prepared to work for a few dollars a day.' It wasn't just the expense of breakdowns, but also the inconvenience of being stranded and having to get it towed home.

'On my first trip with a group of tourists I took them to Dong Ho village which specialises in wood-block prints. I had driven there before so thought I knew the way. But this time it was rice-harvesting season and rice stalks were strewn all along the roadway so that it was hard to see the road, and somehow I missed a small turn on the way back and we ended up 50 kilometres out of our way. Then it started to rain and as the canopy was off, everyone got wet. The second trip had only been going for about fifteen minutes when the jeep broke down outside the Hanoi crematorium and mortuary. The smell was overwhelming and all I could do was bundle my group of tourists into a taxi after refunding their money. The third try was a trip to Tam Dao hill station, only thirty kilometres outside of Hanoi. We made it up the mountain and back down again but the gearbox seized up on the outskirts of Hanoi. I called my mechanic and he came, but I found out that he had blown some of his fingers off with an airgun. There he was trying to fix my gear box with fingers missing from his right hand!'

After that, John only did a couple of weddings and a few airport pick-ups commercially, and then Anh John's Jeep Tours stopped operating. John and Gail used it themselves around town but after three years they finally sold it, going back to riding their motorbikes, which was an easier way to get around Hanoi given the problem of finding somewhere to park a car.

These days John is reinventing himself as an entrepreneur, hoping to be successful in importing ceramics and some ingenious locally crafted bamboo water features into Australia. It has taken a while to set up the legal framework and surmount all the import and export hurdles. And he had a false start with an earlier venture. On a trip to Thailand, John discovered a cheap supply of what he refers to as 'fanny flushers', a hose and nozzle that is fitted to a toilet for use like a bidet, which he thought he could sell successfully to the gay market via the Internet. However, setting up to receive payments via Internet proved more difficult than he thought, advertising in gay magazines more expensive and the freight and import taxes higher than planned. After installing two for his own use and selling one to his ex-wife, John still has 247 of his original order of 250 sitting in his house waiting for the demand to grow.

After more than five years of living in Hanoi, John declares that he never wants to leave. 'In Australia I was never a people person and had few friends. But what I enjoy in Hanoi is "people-ising". I think the women in the North [of Vietnam] are the most beautiful women in the world. So I amuse myself telling women here how beautiful they are and getting big beaming smiles. I love the feel of Hanoi. I love the people. I love being here, as long as I don't have anything to do with the bureaucracy!'

Hanoi, it seems, is the sort of place that smiles benevolently upon and easily accommodates someone like John, allowing him to move from being a prospector, to a successful lacquer artist, a jeep driver, an exporter, or anything else he might dream up.

Stephanie's Story: A New Life

When she was growing up on the large island of Madagascar, Asia never figured in Stephanie's plans or even her imagination. For her, like most people she knew in Madagascar, going abroad meant going to Europe or the United States. Like them, she had no desire to swap living in one developing country for another in Asia, Africa or South America. Yet, when she was twenty-one, Stephanie found herself living in Hanoi and almost ten years later she is still there with no plans for leaving.

Until 1960, Madagascar was, like Vietnam, a French colony. But there are much deeper connections and similarities between the two countries: Madagascans come from Malayo–Polynesian stock and are ethnically related to some of the minority tribes living in Vietnam and other parts of Indochina. They share many of the same customs too; for example, both peoples still worship their ancestors, seek approval from them and have similar ceremonies for those who have died, even though officially the predominant religion of Vietnam is Buddhism and that of Madagascar is Christian. The social order in both societies is conservative. Parents don't easily let go of their children until they are married, the extended family is the most important and influential social group, and 'nice' girls don't talk to foreigners.

Stephanie's mother stayed home to look after the children as was customary at the time. She had three of her own and four nieces and nephews whose mother had died when they were young. Stephanie's father supported the family by working as a shoe designer. Stephanie's family are all practising Catholics and her grandmother's brother is the Cardinal of Madagascar. Stephanie was sent to a Catholic school where nuns taught her. After finishing high school, she studied for three years at a hotel management school.

When she was only fifteen years old, Stephanie met the love of her life, a Madagascan boy only two and a half years older than she was. If he had stayed in Madagascar when Stephanie finished her hotel management training they probably would have eventually married and stayed in Madagascar. Instead, he went to France, with the idea that after a year he would send her a ticket to join him. Although Stephanie describes herself as 'an obedient girl' at that time and 'rather innocent, not knowing much about the rest of the world', she was modern enough to reject this idea. 'I didn't want to be seen to be sitting and waiting for him. I didn't want to hear people say "poor girl" and "are you sure he'll be back?" All I thought was that I can't stay in Madagascar if he's not here and if I have to wait for him then I might as well wait somewhere else.'

At this crucial point, Stephanie's aunt, who was working for UNICEF in Hanoi at the time, invited her to come and stay for six months. At first reluctant, Stephanie was finally pushed into accepting by her father, who said, 'Get out there and find out for yourself.' And so, in October 1994, at twenty-one years of age, fresh out of hotel management school, Stephanie found herself living with her aunt and cousins in Hanoi.

'It took me a year to get to like Hanoi. I was bored and depressed at first. I was away from my city, my family and friends.' After a few months she decided to look for a job for something to do, and through her aunt's contacts found herself working as the food and beverage assistant manager in the Asean Hotel which had just opened.

Stephanie had studied French and English at high school in Madagascar, although she had never practised speaking English before coming to Vietnam. She also spoke some Spanish. But in her new position at the hotel, where she was managing about one hundred Vietnamese staff, she needed to learn Vietnamese. After a one-month formal course in Vietnamese language, she continued to learn on the job and quickly became proficient in her field. But, after about eight months of working at the hotel, she had had enough. Being young and female and trying to manage a large staff of mainly men who were older was not easy. In about September 1995 Stephanie quit her job and returned to Madagascar.

But in the year that she had been away, something had changed in Stephanie. 'When I went back home, I saw life in Madagascar in a different light.' She also realised that it was easier to earn more money in Vietnam than in Madagascar.

At that time, between 1993 and 1996, Vietnam was being talked up as one of the emerging economic dragons of Asia. A foreigner speaking three languages and with experience now in the hospitality industry, Stephanie knew it would be easy for her to find work if she went back to Hanoi. 'I also decided that I couldn't just quit like that!' Her aunt was still working in Vietnam and could provide her with somewhere to live and arrange a visa, and now that Stephanie had had a taste of independence she wanted more. But unlike a lot of foreigners who live in Hanoi for an extended period, Stephanie was not seduced by the charms of the city or Hanoians. 'I had a practical interest only.' And so in early 1996 she headed back to Hanoi for the second time to find a new job and to discover herself.

At the beginning of her stay, Vietnam was just a country that offered Stephanie a better opportunity of earning money and a chance to be more independent. 'As a foreigner in Vietnam I am allowed to do things that I couldn't do in Madagascar. In Madagascar I would never approach a foreigner, I only mixed with other Madagascans. It would be the same if I went to Paris. I would only mix with my own people there.' Stephanie admits that her father was right to push her out of the nest when he did. It was the first time she had left the secure cocoon of her family in Antananarivo, the capital city of Madagascar. 'I didn't know what I wanted to do in life so it was good for me to see different things, to see how other people live and think. And I discovered what it is to live alone. At first I thought, oh my God, what's gonna happen here? And that's when I discovered myself.' But almost nine years after she first arrived in Hanoi, this city became much more special and important to Stephanie, it became the birth-place of her first child.

Once she made the decision to return to Hanoi in early 1996, Stephanie never looked back. She quickly found a job in a French restaurant, and a year later moved to a bar, then a gourmet shop, before settling for four and a half years as food and beverage man-ager at the Sunway Hotel, a newly opened boutique hotel in Hanoi. During that time she enjoyed expatriate life to the full, meeting lots of different foreigners. Stephanie claims that most Vietnamese were not interested in her background and culture. 'Many Vietnamese are not familiar with Madagascar and some think I'm Malaysian, or maybe half black and half Asian. Sometimes I would tell them I am French, but they never believed me.' Her Vietnamese work colleagues introduced her to karaoke in the early days, but she readily admits to being a terrible singer and it wasn't something she enjoyed doing. She tried dancing but found her Vietnamese partners too rigid, although she did introduce monthly dinner-dances at the Sunway Hotel during her time working there, and more recently has been going to salsa classes run by foreigners. Visits outside of the city didn't interest Stephanie either as they only served to remind her of the countryside scenes she had left behind in Madagascar. Visits to pagodas or to meet families of Vietnamese workmates were not as important to her as meeting other foreigners living in Hanoi and enjoying more western-style entertainments. Unlike foreigners from more developed countries who enjoyed the very different and simple life of Hanoi, for Stephanie it was just more of what she was used to back home.

Like most visitors to Hanoi, the first time Stephanie crossed the street she thought she would die. Then she began to ride a bicycle. Later, when her Canadian friend left Vietnam, Stephanie bought her Piaggio motorscooter. 'It took me one and a half hours to travel what should have been a fifteen-minute trip from my friend's place to where I was living, I was so scared. I virtually walked it home with my feet on the ground on either side that first trip. I was frightened of the gears, the speed, the other riders, the lack of rules—everything!' But some practice in a nearby compound soon had her on the road. In wet weather and when she was pregnant, Stephanie used taxis. 'I'm not a good car traveller, as I tend to fall asleep. When I was a baby my parents used to drive me around in the car to put me to sleep, so now when I get in a car I feel sleepy. The taxi drivers here are nice though. I use the same company all the time and they just wake me up when I get home. I couldn't imagine doing that somewhere else, like Paris for example, where I would worry that I would be attacked.'

Towards the end of 2002 Stephanie had enough of working at the hotel and wanted to take a year off to travel around the world on a working holiday. Just before she left though, a friend told her she was leaving her job at an overseas freight company and that Stephanie should apply for it. 'At first I rejected the idea, but later I had second thoughts. I started to think that after being in management positions it might be too hard to go back to casual waitressing jobs as I travelled around the world. And then there was a problem with visas when travelling on a Madagascan passport. Countries like Spain, Italy and the United States had restrictions and required a return air ticket, while I wanted to do it step-by-step and earn enough money as I went. In the end I got tired thinking about it and applied for and was accepted for the job in Hanoi with the freight company. I was also interested to see if I could handle a different sort of job after eight years in the hospitality business. I figured (correctly as it turned out) that it was all about customer service and I knew I was experienced in talking to people and calming them down if they were stressed.' Before embarking on this adventure in her new career, Stephanie decided to head home to Madagascar for a short visit. This decision was to have interesting consequences and set the course for an even bigger adventure than she had bargained for.

Throughout the years, Stephanie's relationship with her teenage love had continued despite distance and only irregular meetings. 'After only about one year together we both said, "I think I want you to be the parent of my children." And while it started like a bit of a joke, we really wanted it as well.' Over the years there had been talk of marriage, but somehow the timing was never right. The first time he proposed Stephanie was too young; later she had just started her job and didn't want to leave it. 'I started to have a different sort of fun and I started to have a mind of my own, which can be difficult for Madagascan men to take. Women are supposed to just follow and support their men.' Nevertheless, something held them together over the years and following their meeting in Madagascar in late 2002, Stephanie went back to Hanoi to start her job as manager of a freight company, unaware that she was pregnant.

According to her working terms and conditions, Stephanie was entitled to four months maternity leave. Under the circumstances, however given that she had only just started her new job, she was worried that if she stayed away more than a few weeks the company would find a replacement and she would lose her job, a job she really needed now. This meant that she didn't have the choice of having the baby in Madagascar or even France or nearby Bangkok. Any of these alternatives would have meant staying away from Hanoi for at least three months, to allow her time to travel before the baby was due and then to arrange a passport for the baby after the birth. So she decided to have the baby in Hanoi at the International Hospital that had been built and run by an Australian company in the mid-1990s and was later taken over by a French operation.

But then, already dealing with being alone in another country, without her extended family or partner for support, the fates dealt Stephanie another blow. At the time her baby was due, the SARS scare came to Vietnam and the French-run International Hospital was closed after discovering an early suspected case of the virus.

Stephanie's mother came to stay with her one month before the baby was due and they went to see the local Vietnamese hospitals that Stephanie would now have to use for the birth of her first baby. 'They looked disgusting, but I told myself, you're not the first one that's going to have a baby. Vietnamese women have babies here every day. You can't think about the bad things, just think, well, you're going to have a baby, it's natural, go for it.'

'I had a beautiful pregnancy. I was dancing until 11.30 p.m. and then eating crabs at a street stall the day before giving birth. The contractions started about 1 a.m. but I wasn't sure at first. I took a shower and then at 1.30 a.m. I woke my mother, called the doctor and met him at the hospital at 2 a.m. The doctor said I had twelve hours to go but I surprised them and gave birth at 6.30 a.m. on 12 July 2003 to a 2.95 kilogram girl. It was a natural birth because they didn't have time to give me an epidural.' Stephanie's doctor was a Vietnamese who spoke English and French and worked at an international medical clinic and was also the Vice-Director of the Hospital for Mothers and Babies. Despite the poor physical facilities, Stephanie had confidence in her doctor and he was always there for her when she needed him.

The labour ward consisted of about thirty beds in one room where those who are in the early stages stay. Opposite, completely visible through a glass divider, is the room where the women giving birth are lined up. 'It is not very reassuring to know you are going to be like that soon.' Stephanie had booked a private room for after the birth but there was no privacy in the delivery process.

However, as a foreigner she was allowed the privilege of having her mother and a friend with her during labour and they massaged her back as she tried to dance and walk herself through the pain. Vietnamese women are not allowed to have husbands or family present with them. 'And they don't know how to deal with the pain. They cry and roll on the floor, there are no mattresses on the beds, the nurses are overworked and the standard of the cleaning is poor. I had to close my eyes. I had to bring my own food and water, everything I needed. After the birth, the hospital was too crowded so I had to share my "private" room. The airconditioner I had paid for didn't work. The room had its own toilet but there was water leaking everywhere and so I couldn't use it. There was no mattress on the bed, just a woven mat. My mother thought I was going to die! I didn't want to eat or drink because I didn't want to use the toilet. It was the middle of summer and there wasn't even a fan. My friends brought a pillow for me. After the birth the nurses don't wash the baby, they just wipe it. The next day they washed her but she came back bright red from crying after the experience. The staff have too many babies to cope with.'

After giving birth at 6.30 a.m., Stephanie was moved to her 'private' room at noon. By 11 a.m. the next morning she was in a taxi on her way home. And she was back in the office three weeks later, having held meetings at her home only four days after the birth. 'It's a man's world,' Stephanie concludes. 'I wish that male bosses had babies and tried to work at the same time.'

Stephanie was lucky that her mother was able to come and stay with her for a year. It was her mother's first time out of Madagascar and while it was like a huge vacation for her because she didn't have the whole family to look after, she became a little homesick. Stephanie, her mum and the new baby moved to a larger house near West Lake, a short distance from the city centre where the air is a bit cleaner and the surroundings a bit quieter. She has a Vietnamese woman to help with the baby and chores. 'I have changed from a social girl who used to go out every night. I haven't suffered any baby blues, I have been too busy!'

As the years have passed Stephanie has seen the rapid development of Hanoi, much faster than that of Madagascar, so that to return home she now considers 'would be like going backwards'. Stephanie says, 'I like my life here in Hanoi—I have a job that allows me to sustain myself and daughter. It is secure to live here and I have met people from many different backgrounds who have given me new ideas. I have also toughened a lot and become very independent. Once my world would have revolved around my partner, but nowadays I am used to being alone and making decisions for myself.'

But, despite living in Vietnam, life there for Stephanie has not been a Vietnamese experience in the sense of immersing herself in Vietnamese culture and social life. 'I like Hanoi, but I don't want to spend the rest of my life here. I have a practical interest only. If I only mingled with Vietnamese I would have stayed the same as in Madagascar. And I didn't make this long trip to stay the same.'

Not long after completing this interview, Stephanie's long-time but distant partner came to Vietnam. Now he and Stephanie and baby Tiana are living happily together in Hanoi and Stephanie's mother has gone back home to her family.

Don's Story:
Fiddling in Hanoi

Don is a thirty-something quietly spoken Scottish architect who has been living in Vietnam since 1997, longer than he has lived just about anywhere else. Don's father worked in the forestry industry in the UK and the family moved every four or five years, which could have contributed to Don's preference as an adult for what he calls a 'vagabond life'. Born in Inverness in Scotland in 1964, Don attended three different primary schools. He did manage to stay at only one secondary school before attending the Dundee Art College in 1981 as an architecture student. Where his interest in architecture came from Don doesn't know. But there was never any question in his mind that an architect was what he wanted to be, and only an architect.

When he was about eleven years old, Don started learning to play the violin. His father had a violin that 'he scratched away on at Christmas and New Year and the rest of the time it stayed in a cupboard', but no-one else in the family played an instrument. At first Don studied classical music with the violin teacher at school, but became more interested in folk music and joined the Highland Reel and Strathspey Society, a group formed in the late nineteenth century for the practice and promotion of Scottish national music.

'Looking back I'm really glad I did that. I wasn't interested in football or other sports. But playing with the group gave me other opportunities.' There were about twenty-five to thirty members in the society, ranging in age from five to seventy-five years. Before they were allowed to play in concerts or on tour they had to memorise all the music. As a thirteen-year-old boy Don travelled overnight by train to London with the group to play with an orchestra in the Albert Hall. 'It was music all the way,' he recalls. Another time the group went to Canada where there is still a strong Gaelic culture in parts. But then, as is often the case, Don stopped playing in his mid teens. 'It wasn't seen as a "cool" thing to do.' At university no-one even knew that he played.

Don's architectural studies took five years of formal training interspersed with three one-year stints of professional practice before taking qualifying professional exams. He worked for firms in Inverness and Edinburgh on a variety of projects, including housing schemes and conversion and restoration projects. Then in 1991, when he was twenty-seven, he took a short holiday in Paris, meeting up with some architecture friends there. This experience convinced him it was time to move on and within two months he had put together his CV and portfolio, cut his ties with Scotland and headed back to Paris intent on finding a job.

After ten days of knocking on doors he had a full-time position with a firm that specialised in conversion work. He stayed with that company for four years, where he worked on some big and interesting projects like the restoration of a building originally designed by Gustave Eiffel and a US$100-million reconstruction of an old chocolate factory which was to become the headquarters of Nestlé.

During this period Don enjoyed life in Paris. He had an apartment close to Pigalle, he spoke French, could fully participate in the social life of the city and he had a good job in a time of recession. He even revived his fiddle playing at this time. Near his office in Paris was a Celtic mission run by a monk from Brittany. It sold the cheapest Guinness in Paris and held traditional Irish music and dancing classes. Don went along with his fiddle and also began playing at friends' weddings and parties, even venturing out into the Paris streets for the famous 21 June Music Festival, where anyone who wants to can take their instrument out into the streets and play.

Despite having a good job and friends in Paris, it wasn't enough to keep Don's wanderlust at bay. Suddenly, after four years, he decided he had had enough and gave three months' notice at work and on his apartment. With no real plans, he bought a one-year round-the-world air ticket in August 1995. His first destination was northern India to meet up with friends who were working there on an aid project, then on to Nepal, Vietnam, Hong Kong to visit friends, New Zealand for Christmas with friends and finally to Australia. After nine months, tired of the travelling and feeling satiated, he went back home for a while, then landed a job in Warsaw for three months. However, when the temperature in December 1996 fell to minus 16 degrees he quickly bought another round-the-world excursion fare and headed off for warmer climates.

Starting with Bangkok, he next called by Ho Chi Minh City in the south of Vietnam for a job interview, but that project fell through. He went on to Australia for six weeks. In March 1997 he went back to Hanoi in Vietnam.

By this time Don was certain that he wanted to stay in Hanoi, but it took him two months to find a job there. He started by getting lists of construction companies operating in Vietnam from the various embassies and then spent most mornings visiting building sites, checking out the work prospects. Most afternoons he would sit at the Au Lac café at the edge of Hoan Kiem Lake in the centre of Hanoi enjoying a coffee and reading the paper. Finally, he got lucky with a six-month contract on the Indonesian joint-venture Horison Hotel construction, which got him his professional start in Hanoi. He still keeps in touch with the Au Lac café staff, who have all moved on now to become young entrepreneurs, bar owners and company directors. When two of the staff married recently, Don was invited to the wedding, which turned into a bit of an Au Lac reunion with another expat regular from the old days coming along, too. But that's the thing about Hanoi—before you know it, you are ensnared and made to feel that you are part of the community.

'After being there for only one day, I wrote in my travel diary "I really like Hanoi". I can't explain why. It wasn't my first experience of an exotic location. I had already been to Nepal and India. I was impressed by the cleanliness and the level of energy I felt in Hanoi. I liked the scale of the city. But mainly, it was something about the genuineness of the Vietnamese people that made it feel so special.' Seven years later, Don still can't define what it is about Hanoi that captured him, except to say that Hanoi feels like home now and he feels part of a community, and he still really likes it.

The old quarter in Hanoi is endlessly fascinating. Originally it consisted of thirty-six streets specialising in different crafts such as Bamboo Basket Street, Paper Votive Street[11], Silver Street, Ladder Street and so on. Many of the streets still retain much of their original character. A walk along Tin Street still assaults your hearing as hundreds of hammers tap away on sheets of tin, shaping boxes and funnels, watering cans and cooking pots. Others, like Silk Street, have gone distinctly up-market, catering for an increasing flow of cashed-up tourists looking to spend on the superb silk fashions and embroidery. On the other hand, the original trades of some streets have almost disappeared and been replaced by stalls selling cheap plastic toys or expensive imported fashions. And jostling for a toe-hold in this busy tourist area are the tour operators, cafes and bars, all squeezing into any available nook or cranny, all trying to capture the tourist trade.

It is a Sunday afternoon. At the end of a very narrow street in the heart of this backpacker territory is a narrow doorway leading into a tiny, tiny bar with about thirty foreigners pressed around the walls. Outside it is pure Vietnam with motorbikes jamming the street, honking horns, conical hats and street sellers. Inside it is pure Irish pub with a fiddler, guitarist, a bass clarinet player, flute player and mandolin player all seated around a drink-laden table playing Irish folk tunes.

Don, to his surprise, is the longest serving member of the group that has come to be known as The Social Weevils, a name whose origin has now been forgotten but was probably inspired by the Government campaign against social evils in Vietnam. Although he had revived his fiddle playing in France and had even taken his fiddle to Poland and played a bit at bonfires in the middle of the Polish forest, he didn't find an opportunity to play in Hanoi at first. Then, in the casual way these things evolve, an expat who had heard a guitarist and violinist playing at a St Patrick's Day party asked them to come along and play for his birthday party on the rooftop of the Saigon Hotel in Hanoi. And a mutual friend invited Don along too and asked him to bring his violin with him. Together for the first time, the three musicians entertained the guests. 'We managed to get through the night, decided we enjoyed it and that we should do it again.' And so began Don's musical adventure in Hanoi.

At first he played a violin he had bought in Hanoi for only US$60, but 'it was like playing a biscuit tin', he laughs 'so I bought one from home'. More than a dozen group members have come and gone over the years, a multinational collection including American, Australian, British, Dutch, Scottish, Canadian and even real Irish players.

Their instruments have been equally diverse, fiddle, guitar, flute, recorder, tin whistle, accordion, mandolin, bodhran, clarinet. 'By chance we discovered a champion Irish mandolin player was living in Hanoi. He had been playing alone for three years, too shy to play publicly until he joined our group.'

Gradually, playing has taken on an increasingly significant role in Don's life. When he was working in Hoi An, he would make a point of coming back to Hanoi at least once a month to play. Now he even travels regularly to Ho Chi Minh City to play some weekends for fun. 'The music scene in Saigon is better and more diverse than the music scene in Hanoi,' says Don. 'As well as expats, there are some good Vietnamese players from the army bands or the symphony orchestra playing Irish music in one Irish bar every weekend. They have learnt from listening to CDs. Technically they are excellent, although maybe they lack some feeling, but there is a Vietnamese tin whistle player from the army band who is outstanding. She sounds like a bird when she plays and moves to the music with real feeling. And there are two expat bodhran players in Saigon.'

Don isn't a person who lives life centre-stage. He usually prefers to remain in the background. And yet, Hanoi worked its magic on him as it has done on many other foreigners, giving him whatever it was he needed to stretch himself and take the brave step of becoming a singer in public. Don jokes that four years of karaoke helped overcome some of his shyness. But it was also that feeling of not being judged, of being comfortable and amongst friends that Hanoi can somehow create. After Peter, one of the originators of the group, returned to Ireland, they were left without a vocalist. Starting off just singing at home or in closed sessions, Don finally overcame his nervousness and began singing in public from the end of 2002. 'I was in the choir at school, but wasn't judged good enough to be in the school musical. So my parents are surprised at my singing. They haven't even heard me sing yet.'

Singing is therapeutic, releasing all those feel-good endorphins! When he first began working in Vietnam though, Don had no such release for his pent-up frustrations while he was working on a Hanoi building site. One of his Vietnamese colleagues once told him, 'Your Vietnamese language is always best when you are shouting at contractors.' In his first job as the person responsible for quality control of the fitting-out stage of a fifteen-storey five-star hotel in Hanoi, Don had many dealings with lots of contractors and hence plenty of opportunity to use his Vietnamese!

'The Horison Hotel looks like a spaceship that has landed on the corner of Cat Linh Street and Giang Vo Street in Hanoi. It is built on the site of an old brickworks and they kept the chimney, so it had a point of interest that none of the other new hotels in Hanoi had. This made it a bit more interesting for me because I had previously worked on an old chocolate factory site in France.' Don was working to a tight deadline. There was a push to have the hotel opened in time for the Francophone Conference being held in Hanoi in October 1997. As it turned out, five of the fifteen floors were opened and fully booked and the public spaces completed before the conference. Don's original six-month contract was extended until the job was finally completed and the hotel officially opened in March 1998.

This was Don's first experience of working on a building site in Vietnam, a very different experience to that of working on buildings in the UK or France. 'Inside the building was like a Beirut bomb-site, with rubbish piled up in corridors and rooms, bricks, plaster, everything. When I showed photos of it to friends they couldn't believe it was a new building; they thought it was a relic from the war.' At the height of building there could be six or seven hundred workers on site. The Japanese contractors were unable to effectively manage the Vietnamese subcontractors, and so cleanliness, protection, safety, and general supervision remained poor for the life of the project. At the end of each floor there were bay windows, just the right size to swing a hammock. One of Don's frequent tasks in the morning was to go around waking up the workers who had already slung their hammocks at the start of the working day. But his main task was to condemn work of poor quality, which meant he was not popular with contractors.

In his first week of work, he experienced the phenomenon of 'loss of face'. Don says, 'I was going from room to room with the contractor and the floor surface on every one of them needed to be condemned, which meant they had to be re-done. The contractor began laughing. I couldn't understand why he was laughing at me. The more he laughed the more upset I became. Finally, someone took me aside and explained that he was in fact embarrassed and that laughing was the Asian response to this sort of situation.'

Safety is a serious problem on building sites and whilst the situation has improved over the years, at that time the Vietnamese paid little attention to it and it was outside Don's responsibility to enforce. Workers might wear a safety harness, for example, but would leave it hanging loose, not clipped. One day a painter fell from the tenth floor to the second-floor pool deck. He was picked up by the workers and loaded into a *cyclo* and taken to hospital. 'I found it shocking,' said Don. 'A report said that he survived but I can't imagine how that could be true. Many of the workers had come to the city from the provinces and hence were not officially considered as being there.'

The lift void posed another danger until safety nets were installed. 'One of the problems was that the toilets were on the second floor, but workers on the fifteenth floor weren't always prepared to run down the stairs to the second floor. One week after installing the safety nets a worker on the fifteenth floor was caught short and decided to squat Vietnamese-style over the void. Unfortunately he lost his balance and, after a triple back flip, landed on the safety net several floors below, trousers around his ankles, some minor injuries to his shoulder, feeling rather embarrassed. But a week earlier and he wouldn't have survived.' At one stage, Don's team of engineers was required to do an inspection of the outside of the building, but when they saw the scaffolding they would have to climb to perform this, they refused. They remained on terra firma and did the inspection from the ground, using a pair of binoculars.

Security was another major problem. One story had it that when a five-star hotel in Hanoi was being built, a tunnel was dug leading from the hotel site under the road to a new housing area where numerous electrical and household fitting shops had suddenly sprung up. When it got to the stage where fittings were being installed in the rooms in Don's hotel, the security was tightened to prevent the theft of the taps, door knobs, light switches and so on. There were 24-hour security guards, electronic and mechanical alarms. Every night Don and his team would check and lock every room and lock access to every floor. They would come the next morning and find rooms gutted, without anybody having seen or heard anything. 'We had these expensive outside light globes. A day after installation they went missing. It turned out that the person with the basket on her head, whom we thought was a bread seller, actually collected the globes and put them in her basket. The police caught her, but then we had to buy our globes back from the police.'

'I'm a Virgo,' explains Don, 'and it's my job to be conscious of details. So, of course it frustrates me here with the work practices, especially when you see materials being damaged before they are even installed, or people stubbing out cigarettes or dropping food on pure wool carpets that have just been laid.' On one occasion though, the workers were too efficient at their job. Don had spent the weekend going through all the bathrooms inspecting the tiles, marking any that were chipped or had bad joints and needed to be replaced. He had marked them all with a water-soluble pen. After he had finished, the cleaners came along and efficiently cleaned all the pen marks from the wall, completely erasing all his hard work. 'It's also amazing how many different trades you can fit in a bathroom in Vietnam,' Don laughs. 'They are on top of each other trying to finish the job, some up in the ceiling, others cutting pipes, installing basins, tiling, painting all at once!'

As the Horison job was coming to an end, Don managed to fit in some part-time work for another company that ultimately won an AusAID-funded contract to renovate a building at the Foreign Languages University in Hanoi, providing him with more work once construction began. During the rest of 1998 and half of 1999, Don worked on and off for a local joint-venture company and did some other small local jobs, fitting out cafes and showrooms, holding on until he could find another big project to sustain his stay.

This appeared in June 1999 when he was offered the job as project coordinator for the Victoria Hotel Group's newest hotel in Vietnam at Hoi An, an old port town near Da Nang in Central Vietnam. Although it meant leaving Hanoi, this new location offered Don another facet of Vietnam and in fact, the job expanded to include working on all of the group's hotels located in SaPa, Ho Chi Minh City, Phan Tiet and Can Tho. Hoi An is a delightful town to visit as a tourist with its ancient streets and houses, Japanese bridge and beautiful beaches. But compared to living in Hanoi it is rather quiet, with few things to do. Fortunately, Don found a refuge to unwind at the end of a hard day's work in a bar and cafe run by three Frenchmen who had previously opened a bar in Ho Chi Minh City. 'Their place became my living room and I would go there most evenings. Other than that, I would go to Hanoi once a month.'

Exhausted after almost two years of intensive work, Don spent a couple of months back in Scotland in the middle of 2001, his first visit in three years. This was followed by a month of lying on a beach in Thailand, recovering from the reverse culture shock of being in the UK. He considered working in Thailand at that time but still wanted to go back to Hanoi to recapture the good experience he had enjoyed there initially.

In April 2002 he was offered a job on the project to build a new international school in Hanoi. This required him to spend two months in Melbourne, returning to Hanoi in July with a team of Australian engineers and architects to set up the project office. Once this project is complete Don will have had a seven year sojourn in Vietnam; his longest stint anywhere ever, and testament perhaps to the seductive charms of Hanoi and Don's determination and persistence.

'There is a certain buzz working on a building site. Every day it seems like chaos, but it works. However, I am becoming tired of being an architect these days, mainly because these projects go on for so long. I prefer to be working on a number of shorter projects going on at the same time.' Don entertains a dream of one day opening his own café, bar or gallery, maybe even an Irish bar in Hanoi. But, he admits it is probably best kept as a dream since he isn't really motivated by business.

For a while Don gave more attention to his interest in photography, something he had enjoyed since university. 'One of the first purchases I made when I started working was a good camera,' Don remembers. 'I enjoyed photographing landscapes, textures and some architecture. I always felt that photographing people was too intrusive.' He continued taking photos in France, but coming to Hanoi inspired him more. There were many things to take his interest here, especially the French colonial and art deco buildings around the city.

In 1998 the company he was working for had an empty shop space below their offices and when they were discussing ways it might be used, it was suggested that Don display some of his photographs there. Suddenly, Don once again found himself centre-stage, not as a fiddler and singer this time but as a photographer, successfully selling his works. 'One of my photos ended up in the Landmine

Foundation office in Washington,' says Don, sounding surprised as well as pleased. Going to Hoi An brought this creative phase to a halt, but Don is gearing up again, inspired by the shadows and light in Hanoi and the idea of photographing the empty moonlit streets. 'I'm not good enough technically to take my photography further and I am not really interested in studying it more. I just like it as a hobby.'

Over the years Don has made some good friends, both expat and Vietnamese. Even though expats are usually transient, it is easy to keep in touch these days with the Internet, and several musical reunions have already been held for past and present Weevils. As far as Vietnamese friends go, Don still has close contact with some of the engineers he worked with on his first project, as well as his Au Lac café friends. 'I have no delusions about being totally accepted in Vietnamese society. I'll never be one of them. But I can be an important part of the team.' The natural friendliness and inquisitiveness of Vietnamese people can easily overcome cultural differences. 'When I returned to Hanoi to live, I went back to the small hotel I had stayed in as a backpacker and was welcomed back into their family.

'Other Vietnamese often laugh at me because they say I have a BaVi accent when I speak Vietnamese.[10] That's probably because the three guys who ran that hotel were from BaVi and would teach me Vietnamese and I would teach them English.' No doubt their English has a strong Scottish flavour too! Other Vietnamese friends who recently married consider Don as an important part of their life and he now finds himself called on to give advice to the couple.

'Living in Vietnam puts you more in tune with your emotions, but the intensity means you need to get away at times. Have you noticed that the traffic is even more erratic at the full moon, and people too?' Don talks about how people in many western countries often seem afraid of making conversation. When his family moved away from Scotland to England they made only one or two close friends. When they moved back north they found people were friendly, chatting at bus stops, saying good morning. Certainly no-one in Hanoi is afraid of making conversation and foreigners are a special focus of interest and attention. Three years after visiting Hoi An as a backpacker Don returned with his parents on holiday and was greeted in a small café with, 'Oh hi, you're back again!' At first Don thought this merely a piece of good PR, but the woman went on to describe the occasion and his companions on the trip.

One of the things Don likes about living in Vietnam is that 'you never know when you wake up what's going to happen'. But also Vietnam allows almost anything to happen, too. Singing was something Don had wanted to do for a long time and Hanoi allowed that to happen. Now people say to him, 'Oh, you're that singer aren't you!' And he exhibited his photographs and people bought them. Things he had never dreamed would happen!

Of the future, Don plans to have some time off when his current job is finished. He doesn't anticipate ever going back to the UK to work as an architect. But he does have plans for enjoying an Irish music festival held in summer on the west coast of Ireland and maybe attending some workshops there, working on his fiddling and generally soaking up the atmosphere. Beyond that, and perhaps a crazy dream of a Scotsman running an Irish pub in Hanoi—or maybe Saigon—he hasn't made plans. Vietnam will always figure strongly no matter what comes next. 'I think I'll always have personal ties with Vietnam. I will always have a reason to come back.'

Endnotes

1. Cochin-China was a former state in southern French Indochina that is now part of Vietnam.

2. A surprise attack by communist forces on South Vietnamese and US forces in January 1968, during the Vietnam War.

3. Kibbutz—a communal agricultural settlement in Israel.

4. In December 1978, Vietnam invaded Cambodia. In retaliation China invaded Vietnam along their common border in February 1979. After one month of hostilities the Chinese declared they had taught the Vietnamese a lesson and withdrew.

5. This building was pulled down in December 1995, leaving a hole in the ground until a modern six-storey plaza was opened in 2002.

6. South-East Asian countries maintained embassies in Hanoi but large scale collaboration was not yet present and membership in ASEAN was a long way away.

7. Trams were introduced into Hanoi in 1899 until the late 1980s. The network ran for 35 kilometres with up to thirty trams operating.

8. The bar first opened in La Thanh Hotel, moved to the Australian Embassy, and the most recent incarnation closed in the spring of 2004.

9. A gyrocopter is a simple one-person helicopter in which the pilot is strapped to a frame.

10. BaVi is a rural area outside Hanoi. People from there, like those in all rural areas of Vietnam, are considered by Hanoians not to speak with the proper Hanoi accent.

11. Paper votives can be fake paper money or small paper replicas of gold bars, cars or motorbikes, or other material possessions that are burnt as a prayer offering.